1390015

Co
9/20/87

A CENTURY OF HORRORS

CROSSCURRENTS

ISI Books' Crosscurrents series makes available in English, usually for the first time, new translations of both classic and contemporary works by authors working within, or with crucial importance for, the conservative, religious, and humanist intellectual traditions.

TITLES IN SERIES

Equality by Default, by Philippe Bénéton, trans. by Ralph C. Hancock
Critics of the Enlightenment, ed. and trans. by Christopher O. Blum
Icarus Fallen, by Chantal Delsol, trans. by Robin Dick
The Unlearned Lessons of the Twentieth Century, by Chantal Delsol,
    trans. by Robin Dick

A CENTURY OF HORRORS

COMMUNISM, NAZISM, AND
THE UNIQUENESS OF THE SHOAH

Alain Besançon

TRANSLATED FROM THE FRENCH BY
Ralph C. Hancock and Nathaniel H. Hancock

ISI BOOKS
WILMINGTON, DELAWARE
2007

Besançon, Alain.
    A century of horrors : communism, Nazism and the uniqueness of the Shoah / Alain Besançon. — [1st English ed.]. — Wilmington, DE : ISI Books, c2007.

        p. ; cm.

        ISBN-13: 978-1-933859-17-0
        ISBN-13: 978-1-933859-18-7 (pbk.)
        ISBN-10: 1-933859-17-2
        ISBN-10: 1-933859-18-0 (pbk.)

        1. Holocaust, Jewish (1939–1945) 2. Communism. 3. National socialism. I. Title. II. Malheur du siècle

D804.3 .B46 2007   2006932518
940.53/18—dc22   0705

                        Originally published as:

Le malheur du siècle: Sur le communisme, le nazisme et l'unicité de la Shoah
                        de Alain Besançon
        World copyright © Librairie Arthème Fayard (Paris), 1998

            English translation published in the United States by:

                        ISI Books
                Intercollegiate Studies Institute
                    Post Office Box 4431
                Wilmington, DE 19807-0431
                        www.isibooks.org

CONTENTS

TRANSLATOR'S PREFACE / page vii

INTRODUCTION / page xiii

CHAPTER 1
PHYSICAL DESTRUCTION / page 1

CHAPTER 2
MORAL DESTRUCTION / page 13

CHAPTER 3
THE DESTRUCTION OF POLITICAL LIFE / page 39

CHAPTER 4
THEOLOGY / page 53

CHAPTER 5
MEMORY / page 71

APPENDIX / page 95

NOTES / page 105

INDEX / page 109

TRANSLATOR'S PREFACE

IT IS HARD to think about the horrors of the twentieth century, but it must be done. By saying that it is hard, I do not mean only that we naturally wish to avert our eyes—from hellish images of huddled, shivering skeletal figures, from the routinization of massive, murderous assaults on civilians, from the dark spectacle of entire anti-civilizations founded on lying and betraying. I mean also that, once we overcome our revulsion in order to consider such horrors, once we manage to expose our own humanity to the challenge of such sophisticated brutalities, it is hard to know what to think, how to assess and evaluate them; it is hard even to know what questions to ask. If Aristotle is at least partly right that we human beings are "political" beings, in the sense of beings whose very nature is accomplished by speaking with each other about what is good and bad, just and unjust—if it is true we can only find a human place in the world by articulating our humanity—then the horrors of the twentieth century make it that much more difficult to be human.

No one has faced this difficulty more soberly, or more lucidly, or with more humanity than Alain Besançon. The compact and trenchant work before you now, first published in French in 1998, may be regarded as the capstone of an edifice of research and reflection whose foundation was laid decades earlier.

Alain Besançon recently retired from the *École des hautes études en sciences sociales* (EHESS; the School of Advanced Studies in the Social Sciences), with which he had been associated since 1965, and where, after 1977, he served as a Director of Studies. He has also taught and pursued research at a number of institutions in the United States, including Stanford's Hoover Institution (1983–84) and Princeton University (1995). He describes himself as, first of all, by formation and inclination, a historian interested in the genesis and meaning of historical realities. The reality that first demanded his attention as a young scholar, and which he has never ceased to investigate and to ponder, is Russia. Ever alert to aspects of the Russian tradition that were exploited by Leninists and other revolutionaries, Besançon is also consistently scrupulous in distinguishing things Russian from things distinctively Soviet. It was in investigating the disturbing transformation of Russia into a revolutionary state founded on Communist ideology that Besançon found it necessary to draw upon the resources of philosophy and theology. And so it is that he was named to the section "Philosophie" of the *Académie des sciences morales et politiques*. Besançon now contributes regularly to the programs of the French *Institut*, of which this *Académie* is a part.

Two of Besançon's works deserve particular notice as background to the present book. In 1977 he published *The Intellectual Origins of Leninism*, which examined with new philosophical depth and precision the nature of the ideological lie that underlay Soviet power. Building in part on the insights of Aleksandr Solzhenitsyn and Raymond Aron, Besançon describes the monstrous power of "ideology," defined as "a systematic doctrine that promises salvation," and vividly depicts the destructive dynamics of a closed system analogous to Gnosticism. Leninist ideology cannot be grasped adequately as another version of Machiavelli's immoral realism, he argues, for the communist lie finally cuts off the believer from all contact with reality. In *The Falsification of the Good: Soloviev and Orwell* (1985), Besançon further explored the character of the evil that is ideology. Here he employs the tools of philosophy and theology to argue that this evil cannot be explained according to the classical notion of a privation of good. Instead, he writes, ideology can only be grasped as a demonic negation of humanity and of reality, a willful denial of what is concretely given.

In the present work, Besançon continues his meditation on the communist evil by comparing it with its "heterozygote twin" (to use Pierre Chaunu's expression), the National Socialist regime. The puzzle that instigates this meditation is the remarkable disparity in the way these two evils are remembered. While Nazism is recognized, justifiably, as the very embodiment of evil, communism somehow benefits from a kind of collective amnesia. It shocks or at least surprises no one today to hear it said that Soviet communism was a good idea that turned out badly, whereas, of course, it would be unthinkable to make a similar observation about Hitler's regime. And yet, as Besançon shows, a sober and unblinking consideration of the two cases, side by side, reveals pervasive similarities.

The Black Book of Communism (1998) has already confronted the world with a statistical comparison between the atrocities of the Nazis and those of the communists (not only Soviet but Chinese, Cambodian, North Korean, etc.). In terms of sheer body count, of course, the devastation wrought by the Leninists far surpasses that of Hitler's minions. But Besançon seeks a richer understanding of the character of the destruction on both sides, physical, moral, and political. In each domain, the author is fully alert to differences between the two camps, but the main effect of the juxtaposition is to convince the reader of their substantial and intricate similarities.

The question of the disparate memories of the two eminent horrors presents itself, therefore, in the author's final chapter, as one fully worthy in itself of the historian's attention. Just how is it that the evil of one tyranny is firmly settled in the popular memory, and that of the other barely registers (especially in Europe)? Here

Besançon acquits himself admirably as a historian, fully explaining this disparity without explaining it away—that is, without removing our sense of scandal at such a yawning gap between truth and public perception. He even leaves us with some hope that this gap might someday be narrowed.

I will not attempt to summarize the culminating point of Besançon's meditation on ideological evil (in chapter 4, "Theology"), in which he finds it necessary to recur to—how shall I say, the deepest? or the most elemental?—of religious notions. The reader may be left puzzled, as well as shaken, by the author's laconism at this critical point in his analysis. One might reasonably have hoped for more discussion of such an essential question as that of the deepest motivation of murderous ideologues. Or, one might judge, on reflection, that little more can be said of the mystery of evil, and that no one should be asked to peer any longer into such an abyss.

Alain Besançon's distinctive voice struck me in my first reading of this book, and it deeply impresses me still. Calm and careful in surveying the dreadful comparison between communist and Nazi evil, the author is at the same time engaged to the depths of his humanity. In contemplating the massive horrors of a century coming to a close, he is somehow clear-sighted, almost serene, yet without detachment from his, or the reader's, humanity. I wanted to translate this book for an English-speaking audience because Alain Besançon helped me, by his example, to begin to grasp what it might mean to be human, to be aware of and to live up to our humanity, after the twentieth century.

AMONG THE NUMEROUS debts that might be acknowledged here, I must at least mention these: The author, Alain Besançon, was unfailingly and graciously obliging in responding to all queries on points of translation or information where my own knowledge was lacking. Our mutual friend, Daniel Mahoney, provided encouragement and very concrete assistance from beginning to end. Uzoma Chukwu and Julie Johnson of the Monterey Institute of International Studies reviewed a major part of this translation meticulously and expertly, and provided numerous very useful suggestions. The unusually skillful editors at the Intercollegiate Studies Institute helped us catch mistakes and improve clarity. Bryan Benson also provided a helpful review of an early draft. Finally, let me express my gratitude for the opportunity to work with my son and cotranslator, Nathaniel—a skilled craftsman, and a good man.

Ralph C. Hancock
Provo, Utah
February 2007

INTRODUCTION

THIS ESSAY RAISES two interrelated questions. It does not claim to answer them exhaustively. The first deals with historical awareness, which, today, appears to me to be seriously divided. The disagreement concerns what most characterizes the twentieth century compared to all others: the extraordinary scale of the massacre of men by men, which was made possible only by the rise to power of Leninist communism and Hitlerian Nazism. These "heterozygous twins" (Pierre Chaunu), despite being enemies and emerging from dissimilar histories, share several common traits. Their goal was to achieve a perfect society by uprooting the evil that hindered its creation. They claimed to be philanthropic because they sought the good—one of all mankind and the other of the German people—and because this ideal gave rise to enthusiastic devotion and heroic acts. But what they have most in common is that they arrogated themselves the right—and even the duty—to kill, and they both did so with similar methods, on a scale unknown in history.

Today, however, historical memory does not treat them equally. Although Nazism completely disappeared more than half a century ago, our abhorrence of it is not at all weakened by time, and rightly so. Our horrified reflection on Nazism seems to even gain in breadth and depth each year. Communism, on the other hand, although still fresh and just recently fallen, benefits from an amnesia and an amnesty that receive the almost unanimous consent, not only of its supporters—because they still exist—but of its most determined enemies, and even its victims. Neither side judges it fitting to bring it back from oblivion. Sometimes Dracula's coffin opens halfway. This is what happened at the end of 1997, when a book (*The Black Book of Communism*) dared to tally the deaths that could be attributed to communism. The book suggested a range of 85 to 100 million. The scandal was short-lived and the coffin is already closing again—without, however, anyone seriously contesting these figures.

I recently had the opportunity to study this contrast between the amnesia concerning communism and the hypermnesia concerning Nazism. I addressed it briefly from the rather narrow point of view of the historical and political conditions that might explain why communism has been forgotten.[1] The subject needed a more detailed examination that includes other viewpoints. This is the purpose of the first part of this essay.

The second question relates to the Shoah. To what degree, in the context of the century's tremendous slaughter, must it be considered distinct? Can one consider it as just one tomb among others within the general cemetery? And if not, why not?

That the Shoah haunts the historical consciousness of the century in general, and the relationship or comparison between the memory of communism and that of Nazism in particular, is easier to point out than to explain. I had felt this strongly myself during my speech as I emphasized why the Jewish people had taken responsibility for the memory of the Shoah: out of a moral obligation linked to the long memory of persecutions; out of a religious obligation linked to Job-like praising and impassioned questioning of the Lord who promised to protect his people and who punishes crime and injustice. Humanity has Jewish memory to thank for reverently preserving the records of the Shoah. The enigma lies in the fact that there are peoples who have forgotten.

The difficulty stems from the fact that, in order to answer the second question, one must move to another level. Communism and Nazism can, indeed, be considered two species of the same genus, the *ideological* genus. Their appeal, the nature and mode of their power, and their type of crime stem from the mindset upon which they entirely depend: ideology. By this term I mean a doctrine that, in exchange for conversion, promises a temporal salvation that claims to conform to a cosmic order whose evolution has been scientifically deciphered and requires a political practice aimed at radically transforming society. One might push the comparison between communism and Nazism even further, noting their differences and similarities, without leaving the realm of historical and political analysis.

On the contrary, with the Shoah we immediately leave that realm. Even though politics, particularly in France, attempts to make the Shoah an issue, to force it into the endless struggle between the "right" and "left," this catastrophe is on an entirely different level, like a very solemn and burning hearth that is self-sustaining, far from the struggles of the public square. Our consciousness of the Shoah does not fit within a purely political analysis; it is ill at ease with making the Shoah the object of comparative, neutral, "scientific" study. It maintains the ineffable sense of an event that is unique in this century and in all of time, requiring something other than objective study: a special reverence, a sacred silence. We are no longer in the history of ideology, but in the history of religion— even in religion itself, the Jewish religion initially, and as a result, the Christian religion.

The fact remains that the two questions—the comparative historical awareness of the two murderous ideologies and the awareness of the Shoah—are linked. The sense of the uniqueness of the Shoah emerged slowly from the confused memory of Nazism. This is not unrelated to the different treatment reserved for communism.

It is risky to deal with two series of events that differ in nature and are separated by time and space, but that history has nevertheless obscurely connected. In order to clarify this obscurity to the best of my ability, I briefly trace the genealogy of the problem. Next, I make a step-by-step comparison of communism and Nazism from the point of view of the destruction they have caused in the physical, moral, and political realms. I confess that, having already dealt with the subject extensively, I had really hoped—because it is so distressing—not to revisit it. But circumstances brought me back. I then venture into theology to try to locate exactly the uniqueness of the Shoah. I conclude in favor of uniqueness, but realize that agreement on the meaning of this uniqueness is unlikely in the foreseeable future.

THE ISSUE OF the uniqueness of the Shoah, of which I think the victims were immediately aware, did not fully emerge into public consciousness until several years after the event. Primo Levi's *Se questo è un uomo* (*If This Is a Man*), now universally recognized as one of the most moving accounts of Auschwitz ever written, was penned the moment the author returned to Italy. It was turned down by several major publishers, but published all the same in 1947 when a small company printed 2,500 copies of the work. The company soon went bankrupt, and the book fell into oblivion. It was republished by Einaudi in 1958, and the fame it gained was so well deserved that its previous obscurity exposes one aspect of the enigma. "In this difficult postwar period," Levi explains, "people were not overly eager to relive the painful years which had just passed." The analysis is accurate, but it is vague and insufficient. In the aftermath of the war every deportation camp evoked the same horror, and the distinction between forced-labor camps (such as Buchenwald) and death camps (such as Treblinka) was not clearly made. Everyone felt sorry for the victims; no one thought to distinguish between categories. At the Nuremberg trials, people referred only to the "persecution" of the Jews. In reading Primo Levi, it is evident that in his camp and his commando (work team) the Jews occupied the very last circle of hell; but there were other circles, composed also of non-Jews—there were many in Auschwitz—and every prisoner, including the most criminal Kapo, was denied the quality of being human. This is the metaphysical core of the book, already announced in the title. As with any event that surpasses the imagination, the deportation went through an amnesic phase—or a phase combining amnesia and aphasia—which spared neither the prisoners nor the surviving Jews among them. The unspeakable is not easily said. It was time that made it possible to bring into focus this subject which cannot be apprehended directly.

But in order for the topic of the Shoah's specificity, of its *uniqueness,* to attain general historical consciousness, a great event had to take place. A second event was also necessary for the topic of the *comparison* between Nazism and communism to reach this consciousness.

THE FIRST EVENT involved a considerable increase in the "visibility" of the Jewish people. The Jews were emancipated during the nineteenth century, and, like other religious groups, they were granted their religious rights, the freedom of "Israelite worship." They were not, however, given specific civic rights. Since biblical times, Judaism has always been understood as inextricably both a religion and a people. Sometimes this second half of Jewish identity had to be abandoned, even forgotten, in Western democracies; at other times, it had to be carried like a burden in countries where the modern concept of citizenship had not erased the concept of "ethnic character." Nazism had replaced the concept of people with the concept of race, and it had excluded this particular "race" from mankind. In postwar Europe, the concept of a "Jewish people" no longer had any foundation. In the Western world, there were citizens—English, French, Italian, etc.—who were Jewish because of their "origins" or confession. In the communist world, the Jewishness of the Jews was theoretically destined for obliteration, and in the meantime, it was forbidden to claim it.

There was a third element in Jewish consciousness: land. In 1948 the Jewish people appeared to the world in the modern form of a largely secular national state, enjoying the total independence that they had lost during the Assyrian and then Babylonian conquests, and a territorial presence that had been all but wiped out from the time of the Jewish wars of Titus and Hadrian. Thanks to the Law of Return, the Hebrew state established itself as the rightful homeland of all the Jews throughout the world.

The countries under communist domination recognized the state of Israel for varying political reasons. Democratic countries had more reliable reasons for recognizing it, because, aside from political motives, what might be called religious motives were at work. The Christian world was beginning to develop a sense of guilt, which was to grow further. Religious consciousness of Jewishness, which had been obscured over the centuries by the direction taken by the interpretation of the Scriptures and the teaching of the Church Fathers, was reemerging and beginning to ferment in the Catholic world. This was the starting point of an enormous reversal, of which Vatican II was only a stage, a reversal that is not yet complete.

Thus, in most instances, the Western world rather easily accepted the new self-image that the Jews had developed of themselves as a result of the founding of Israel. In particular, the West accepted that the Jews, who have always had a deep sense of patriotism towards their various diasporic homelands, might develop a second patriotism directed towards Israel, albeit a patriotism informed by a different feeling and a different kind of loyalty. One might well compare this right of double patriotism—which public opinion would not have granted to other minorities—to the equally exceptional, precarious, and in this case purely religious privilege of exemption from imperial worship and civic religion obtained by the Jews around the time of Herod the Great.

This new awareness of Jewish identity developed spontaneously and gradually. Nevertheless, one important year should be mentioned: 1960. Until then, Israel's patriotic feelings thrived on memories of the armed resistance to Nazism. The insurrection of the ghetto of Warsaw was more willingly evoked than the passively experienced genocide. The Eichmann trial, which Israeli authorities hoped would cause a public stir, marked a change of course. The Shoah became a central and, in some respects, foundational event, a basis of legitimacy. It was the starting point for a legal, moral, philosophical, and theological debate in which illustrious minds from around the world (Hannah Arendt, Raymond Aron, and Gershom Scholem) became involved, a debate to which there is no end in sight.

In 1956 the second event, the Khrushchev report, made comparison inevitable. As early as 1917, Bolshevik communism was known to be a criminal system. But because of the vast influence of the idea, and the power of misinformation and deceit of the movement's organs, this knowledge was not verified. It was denied in good faith by a multitude of honest people.

The Nazi secret involving the destruction of the Jews of Europe was a "simple" secret secured by conventional means: isolated extermination centers, periodic execution of subordinate agents taken from among the victims, the oath binding the exterminating groups, and their relatively small numbers. The Bolshevik secret was more complicated. It also included a military and police element that was simple and conventional. However, this small group was protected by an extremely thick ideological fog in such a way that even if the secrecy protecting the operations of destruction were penetrated, the leak would be sealed up by a general unwillingness to believe the revelation, and the barrier would soon be airtight once again. There were times—for example, between the Spanish war and the victory over Nazism—when knowledge about communism no longer existed beyond its borders, except in the minds of certain individuals. These were usually former communists who had personally experienced it, or disappointed and appalled former leftists who, for the most part, were incapable of passing on their knowledge and often incapable of thinking matters through to the end.

Until 1956 the broken chain of accounts, despite being documented and irrefutable, remained localized and devoid of authority among scholars—the guardians of critical thinking—and among politicians, even those foreign and hostile to the idea of communism. Lending their credibility to such accounts would have required them to undertake a vast revision of their worldviews, because these accounts (the same was true for emerging reports of Nazism) painted an improbable universe, one based on a disconcerting logic, and finding their bearings would have required strenuous effort. Moreover, they did not feel threatened. For example, shortly before 1950 people were scandalized by David Rousset's claim regarding Soviet camps. Sartre had no trouble arguing that, because the concept of a camp is philosophically contradictory to the concept of socialism, these camps could not have existed. During the Kravchenko trial of 1948, Mrs. Buber-Neumann provoked an outcry when she affirmed that remnants of law survived in the German labor camp that did not exist in the Soviet camp where she had been imprisoned before Stalin handed her over to Hitler.

The Khrushchev report did not show the slightest remorse to noncommunist victims of communism. The only true crime of the Stalinist system, the crime that fills it with indignation, was that it carried out large-scale executions of communists who were loyal to the cause. However, even so incomplete a confession introduced a decisive weakness in the brittle ideological structure. According to the secretary general, crimes against noncommunists were really only blameworthy because they handicapped the project and weakened communist power. But after the report, people began asking questions about the crimes committed by communists. The system became the object of general examination and a legitimate suspicion that was now impossible to put a lid on. The investigation grew, yet feebly and intermittently, because communist power lingered on for about thirty more years, a period of time almost as long as the one that separated communism from its birth. Throughout this entire time communist authorities maintained a position of total denial, even while they slowly proceeded to dismantle the camp system. *The Gulag Archipelago* (1974) acted as a battering ram that came crashing into the back door of the lie. But it was only a book: there was still no smoking gun. No one anywhere on earth had seen or touched communist camps except their few survivors. The Cambodian mass graves were the exception. Despite everything, one could say that at the moment of the collapse the secret's seal was broken—although communist revisionism remains much stronger than in the case of Nazism.

THUS, IN THE mid-1960s the horrors of the century, Nazism and communism, were both indicted together. But were they indicted for the same crime? This is the focus of the discussion that follows.

I have divided the discussion into several segments, which is not without its drawbacks because compartmentalizing can cause one to lose sight of the unity of the subject. I will examine the question from the angle of destruction. Indeed, the only elements of Nazism and communism that remain are those which withstood them, such as "dissident" literature. The rest is a field of ruins to excavate and clean up. The destruction was material: living people were converted into corpses. It was moral: honest, rational souls became criminal, insane, and stupid. It was political: the structure of society was violated and then remolded according to the ideological project. Then, leaving the realm of historical analysis, the same investigation must be undertaken from a philosophical and theological point of view. Finally, I will revisit the subject of my speech at the French Academy and describe the work of memory. I will conclude with the uniqueness of the Shoah.

CHAPTER 1
PHYSICAL DESTRUCTION

SIX NAMES

Before making any comparison between the communist and Nazi experiences, six names must be mentioned: Auschwitz, Belzec, Chelmno, Majdanek, Sobibor, and Treblinka. These were the six centers of the industrial extermination of the Jews. The typical sequence of events was the following: transportation; sorting on the train's arrival; tattooing; immediate transfer of women, children, and those unfit for work to the gas chamber or mass grave. To my knowledge, this sequence did not exist in the communist world. These six names cannot be mentioned without bringing to mind the documents, eyewitness accounts, studies, reflections, poems, songs, and prayers that attempted to communicate the incommunicable. It is from this absolute—and, to use a metaphor, from this absolute zero taken as the *terminus a quo* of all subsequent measures—that the physical destruction wrought by the communist regime might be assessed.

Raul Hilberg wrote a scrupulous, verified, and infinitely documented survey, *The Destruction of the European Jews.*[1] Like Primo Levi, he had a difficult time finding a publisher, and his survey was not published until 1985. There is no work that describes communist destruction so accurately and in so much detail, and such a work will not be possible for a long time. I will borrow Hilberg's outline of Jewish destruction to analyze communist destruction.

According to Hilberg, the destruction of the Jews of Europe occurred in five stages:

> expropriation
> concentration
> "mobile slaughter operations"
> deportation
> execution at specially designated centers

Using the same framework, we observe that communist destruction incorporated the first four means, but with variations. In keeping with its nature and project, communism omitted the fifth stage and added two others—judicial execution and famine— that Nazism did not need.

We shall address each stage in turn.

EXPROPRIATION

Expropriation was the first measure communist authorities employed. Because communism is defined in part by the idea that social evil has its roots in private property, expropriation of the "means of production" was immediate. But because people had to be torn away from the idea of property and thoroughly subjugated to the new power, expropriation of housing, bank accounts, land, and livestock logically followed. People retained hardly more than their clothing and furniture.

There have always been wealthy people in communist countries, but these were not to be called "owners." Some "illegally" possessed rare goods; others were privileged, as a reward for their political loyalty and by virtue of their position in the system, to enjoy "advantages." Due to their link to private property, rights disappeared altogether: all that remained were "judicial" formulations of party decisions. As for Nazi Germany, expropriation and the removal of legal protections hit only Jews at first. "Aryans" still enjoyed rights and property, although these rights were restricted, residual, and—according to the logic of the system—destined to disappear.

CONCENTRATION

Screening and categorizing were not implemented in the communist regime as they were in the Nazi one. Nazism viewed Jews as though their very physical beings were individual sources of infection. It was thus necessary to pursue them as in a rodent or mosquito control operation, to search them out in any corner where they could be hiding. To the fulfillment of this task, the regime allotted money, personnel, and meticulous effort. Communism set itself a task that was more vague and shapeless, hence more extensive. Communism had to destroy "the enemy of socialism," "the enemy of the people." First, it was necessary to neutralize the designated institutional enemy: whether the wealthy, the nobles, the bourgeois, the capitalists, the well-to-do peasants, etc. Next were those who might harbor hostile feelings: feelings "outside the line," even feelings of mere indifference. Members of this group could be identified within the "proletariat," the "middle class" peasantry, the "poor," and the "progressive" intelligentsia. They were also found in the party, the army, and the police force. Because communism's hidden enemies had no visible features, no physical marks such as circumcision, and because they did not belong to any well-defined community or lineage, they had to be identified, made to confess their hidden thoughts and treacherous intentions, before they could be "eliminated." This required a much more significant and sustained effort. That is why the communist regime had more police and repressive organs than those established to pick out Jews and bring them to the concentration sites. A few thousand police officers were sufficient for the needs of the Gestapo, compared to the almost 500,000 officers required by the KGB. In the German Democratic Republic alone, the Stasi (Ministry for State Security) employed many more than the Gestapo had in all of Germany and occupied Europe.

According to Hilberg, two years (1941–42) were all that were needed to implement the "Final Solution" for almost three-fifths of the targeted population. For the Soviet "forces," by contrast, the task was never finished. From November 17, 1917, until the last day of the Soviet regime, the entire population had to be sorted, accounted for, recorded, screened, and rescreened.

"MOBILE SLAUGHTER OPERATIONS"

Hilberg reports that approximately one-fourth of the Jews murdered (and perhaps more) were killed by special units: by the *Einsatzgruppen* and *Kommandos* that advanced behind the regular troops. These units executed their victims on the spot, usually with machine guns. The Wehrmacht units would sometimes follow suit.

Such "mobile slaughter operations" were also used heavily by communist regimes. Open-air slaughter accompanied the Red Army's recapture of the Ukraine, the Caucasus, Siberia, and central Asia. The slaughter that began with the Peasant War in 1919 and lasted until the New Economic Policy (NEP) in 1921 was both massive and systematic. The Red Army spared no means: they used tanks and poison gas against the peasants, who were being expropriated and starved, and against the Cossacks, who were almost wiped out as a people. A 1923 book by Vladimir Zazoubrine describes the operations of a local Cheka.[2] Trucks delivered people to be killed, impersonal mass executions were conducted in large basements by bullets to the back of the head; after the bodies had been removed, the next fleet of trucks arrived. Open-air executions resumed during collectivization, and gas vans were used during the Great Purge. In China, ruthless open-air executions took place several times: during the first two years following the communists' seizure of power, in the era of the "Great Leap Forward," and then during the Cultural Revolution.

Open-air executions also took place in Korea, Vietnam, and Ethiopia, but Cambodia was the hardest hit by them. Due to the lack of modern equipment, the slaughter there was carried out with knives, hammers, machetes, and clubs. Often, the executioners were children whom Angkar had chosen to educate by enabling them to perfect their skills in torture. The mass graves of this period are currently being excavated.

DEPORTATION

Deportation to labor camps was invented and systematized by the Soviet regime. Nazism only imitated it—the word *Lager* (camp) is common to the Russian and German languages. The first camps were opened in Russia in June 1918, about six months after Lenin and his party seized power.

Soviet deportation was a more sweeping and complex phenomenon than Nazi deportation. In Germany, there were informal differences between camps with a comparatively low death rate (Dachau) and camps with such a high death rate (Dora) that they bordered on extermination camps. In the Soviet Union, the range was greater and the categories more clearly separated.

For the Soviet Union, three categories of deportation can be distinguished. The first entails the deportation of entire peoples— Tartars, Chechens, Germans of the Volga Region, etc.—or entire "social" categories, such as the ten million "Kulaks." The greatest number of deaths occurred during transport, which occurred in more or less the same conditions as those of the Nazi deportation trains, but over much greater distances. The second greatest number of deaths took place during the first year, when the deportees ended up in the central Asian steppe or in a Siberian taiga or tundra without warm clothes, farming tools, or seeds. In some cases, everyone died: deportees, guards, and dogs. A 50 percent mortality rate is generally ascribed to this type of deportation. Deporting peoples appears to have been a peculiarly Russian practice; we have no accounts of it for other communist zones—whether because they lacked the space or because ethnic heterogeneity did not complicate the socialist plan. The brutal and murderous transfer of Germans out of Poland and Czechoslovakia just after World War II can also be included in this category.

The second category encompasses deportation to the labor camps. The gulag became a massive administrative structure that was standardized in the 1930s and was capable of managing a significant portion of the country's workforce (11 percent has been suggested). The abundant gulag literature offers a description similar to that of the Nazi labor camps. It speaks of the wake-up call, the labor *commando,* the food rations proportionate to the so-called "norm," the hunger, the blows, the torture, the executions. Indeed, the day-to-day life for Shalamov in Kolyma precisely mirrored that of Primo Levi in Auschwitz. The concrete details were the same: the widespread stealing, the principle of every man for himself, the physical exhaustion, the slow—or even rapid—moral degradation, the same bunkers, the same wooden planks for beds, the same sleep, the same dreams. The exhausted detainee who could no longer hold his own and was about to die was referred to as a "Muslim" in the Nazi camp and as a *dokhodiaga* in the Soviet camp.

There were of course some variations, which stemmed from the degree of organization and the climate. In Auschwitz a bell was used to wake people, whereas in Kolyma someone would strike a piece of rail. Here, the dead were not incinerated in a crematorium: in the wintertime, the frozen bodies were simply piled up in rows with labels attached to the big toes, and there they remained until their graves could be dug. In the vast archipelago of camps located in northeast Siberia, the horror of the cold, the desolate landscape, and the infinite distance that separated the camps from the inhabited world added to the despair. In certain camps, the death rate was as high as 30 or 40 percent per year. Considering the duration of the sentences and the longevity of the Soviet regime, this approached extermination—though an immediate extermination that left nothing to "chance" was not witnessed there as it was in Treblinka.

As for the third category: around the actual gulag was a zone of forced labor and monitored residence for those employed at large work sites, dams, canals, and secret military arsenals. The boundaries were blurred, then: after all, no one enjoys freedom in communist regimes. That is why, when Bukovsky was asked, "How many prisoners are there in the USSR?" he could jokingly reply: "270 million."

Camps existed throughout almost the entire area of communist domination. In Romania, for example, the Danube–Black Sea Canal labor site resulted in perhaps 100,000 deaths; in fact, it was the burial ground of former elites. Fragments of information on the Vietnamese and Chinese camps (the *Laogai*) have also emerged. A former Soviet *zek* told me the following story: a prisoner from the *Laogai* who had escaped to Siberia believed he had reached paradise when he was thrown in my witness's camp! Whereas the gulag had given him a definite sentence, his detention in China had been of indefinite duration, with release to be determined by his "moral progress" (the Chinese camps were considered a "school"). Further: at night he was returned to the Soviet barracks, whereas in China he had been chained to his labor site. As for North Korea, the little that is known about the camps there is spine-chilling. They are currently in full operation.

JUDICIAL EXECUTION

Two methods of execution were employed regularly by communism and only when deemed necessary by Nazism. The first is judicial execution.

Nazis did not carry out judicial executions on Jews because, in the Nazi view, the Jews did not belong to the human race and thus were not worthy of any "justice." Nazism employed judicial executions on its opponents, resistant fighters, and supporters, after a more or less summary but realistic examination of the facts.

Under communism, executions (firing squads, bullets to the back of the head, hangings) theoretically had to originate in a judicial investigation. This happened so that the "people" or their representative (an organ of the party) could identify and convict the avowed or hidden enemy. The executions, which were summary in the early days, gradually acquired a judicial character as the system (the *prokuratura*) became refined. During the period known as "The Great Terror," which began in 1934, confessions were highly prized and obtained by any means necessary, including the simplest and most widely used one: torture.

The distinctive feature of this period was that most of the persons arrested—often in order to reach a preset arrest quota—were not at all connected with the charges against them. Either they were passive and incapable of even conceiving of any opposition, or they were sincere communists who possessed all the required love and veneration for Stalin. This was the root of the agonizing fear that weighed upon the entire population. It was also the root of a feeling of insanity, of being caught in a living nightmare—the people never managed to see the logic of this vast crushing, killing machine. People expected to be arrested because they saw their neighbors silently disappear, and they listened for footsteps coming up the stairs at night, keeping a prisoner's bundle of belongings under their beds. Most of the communist countries, the popular democracies of Europe and particularly of Asia, lived through such periods. The notion that Hitler inspired the "Great Terror" is not entirely unfounded: the "Night of the Long Knives," the blitz-purge conducted by the Nazi Party in 1934, claimed about eight hundred victims. But Stalin's purges claimed more than a thousand times as many.

FAMINE

Unlike ordinary food shortages, which are a constant feature of human societies, famine has been a recurrent specter of communist regimes. It has been observed in the USSR, China, Ethiopia, and Korea.

Most of the time, famine was a consequence of communist politics. At the heart of communism lay the principle that control must extend over all subjects. The possibility that peasants might organize themselves spontaneously outside the party was intolerable. And so they were expropriated and forced into the artificial surroundings of the *kolkhoz*, the popular commune. This inevitably caused a shortage of crops. One cannot say that the party exactly wanted famine, but rather that this was the price it was willing to pay to attain its political and ideological objectives. And pay it did: in Kazakhstan, the population fell by half.

However, there were also cases for which famine was deliberately planned with the specific goal of extermination. This was the case in Ukraine in 1932 and 1933. The goal was not to put an end to any peasant resistance—collectivization had already crushed it—but to put an end to the existence of the Ukrainian nation. The killing in Ukraine has been referred to as genocide—and rightly so.

Whether accepted as a means or willed as an end, famine was the communists' most murderous method of human destruction. It accounted for more than half of the deaths attributable to the communist system in the Soviet Union, and for approximately three-quarters of those deaths in China.

NAME AND ANONYMITY

As for the Jews exterminated by Nazism, the number is known with a precision that is constantly refined by research and by Jewish piety. Directories indicating the total number of passengers and the departure date of each train are available for consultation. Names are carefully listed and preserved. Of the people exterminated by communism, by contrast, the estimate's margin of error is in the range of several tens of millions. The range deemed acceptable by the *Black Book*, for example, spans from 85 to more than 100 million.

This terrible discrepancy means that some who were exterminated like animals were honored as men, and others who were killed in a way that was perhaps more humane (in the sense that they were at least attributed "enemy" status) were forgotten like animals. But the difference arises not only due to the piety or impiety of memory; it also stems from the fact that conducting surveys is impossible or banned in almost the entire area that was or is under communist rule. In addition, it stems from a general will to amnesia in the case of communism and to hypermnesia where Nazism is concerned. And it stems, finally, from the distinct natures of Nazism and communism. Whereas Nazism operated on a succession of established, administratively definable categories—disabled persons on the eve of the war, Jews, Gypsies, etc.—communism carried out ill-defined, simultaneous, random decimations that could affect the entire subjugated population.

THE MODE OF killing is not a criterion of evaluation. The temptation to judge one death as innately more terrible than another must be resisted: no death can be seen from the inside. No one can know what a child experienced while inhaling Zyklon B gas or while starving to death in a Ukrainian *isba*. Because people were killed without any form of justice, one must exclaim that they all perished terribly—one person as much as the next—because they were innocent. Only when justice is present can one deem some executions more honorable than others—death by the sword, for example, more honorable than death by hanging. But because the idea of honor was foreign to the exterminations of the twentieth century, it is impossible and indecent to rank the forms of torture.

CHAPTER 2
MORAL DESTRUCTION

THE PHYSICAL DESTRUCTION—the vast loss of life and demolition of the earth that constitute the most obvious aspect of the century's ideological disasters—tends to be the focus of the studies and statistics. But surrounding this is an invisible sphere where the damage is probably more extensive, affects more people, and will take even longer to repair: the destruction of minds and souls.

INEPTITUDE

The intellectual genealogy of the two main ideologies that engulfed part of humanity in the twentieth century can be traced—and this has been done. The danger is that one might come to believe that the vast, deep-seated ideas upon which these ideologies drew live on in those ideologies. But this would grant them a dignity and nobility they do not deserve, would play their game—for this is the genealogy to which they lay claim. Marxism-Leninism proclaimed itself heir to a tradition stretching back to Heraclitus and Democritus. It claimed to descend from Lucretius, the Enlightenment, Hegel, and the entire scientific movement. It claimed to be a synthesis and a fulfillment of these movements. Nazism found its predecessors in Greek tragedy, Herder, Novalis, a different reading of Hegel, and Nietzsche; and naturally, it based its legitimacy on the scientific movement since Darwin. Yet these claims must not be believed. They constitute an illusion entailing the further danger of compromising the lineage to which they lay claim: there is a risk of criticizing Hegel—or any other philosopher or scholar—for having begotten such descendants.

This illusion wears off when we observe how the Nazi and communist leaders truly operated intellectually. Their thinking was completely governed by an extraordinarily impoverished system of interpreting the world. It saw classes or races as engaged in a dualistic struggle. The definition of these classes or races makes sense only within the system, with the result that any objectivity that could exist in the notion of classes or races vanishes. These notions gone awry explain the nature of the struggle; they justify it and, in the mind of the ideologist, guide the actions of enemies and allies. The means used to reach the goal can be cunning and shrewd (and in fact, with Lenin, Stalin, Mao, and Ho Chi Minh, communism benefited from agents more capable than Hitler). But the logic of the system as a whole remains absurd, and its goal unattainable.

The psychological state of the militant is distinguished by his fanatical investment in the system. This central vision reorganizes his entire intellectual and perceptual field, all the way to the periphery. Language is transformed: it is no longer used to communicate or express, but to conceal a contrived continuity between the system and reality. Ideological language is charged with the magical role of forcing reality to conform to a particular vision of the world. It is a liturgical language for which every utterance points to its speaker's adherence to the system, and it summons the interlocutor to adhere as well. Code words thus constitute threats and figures of power.

It is not possible to remain intelligent under the spell of ideology. Nazism seduced some great minds (Heidegger, Carl Schmitt), but these projected onto Nazism foreign ideas of their own: a profound antimodernism and antidemocratism, and nationalism transformed into metaphysics. Nazism seemed to take on all these elements—but not the reflection, depth, and metaphysics that made them of value to the intellectual lives of these philosophers. They, too, had succumbed to the illusion of genealogy.

Marxism-Leninism recruited only second-rate minds (Georg Lukács, for example): men who lost their talent rather quickly. Communist parties could boast a number of illustrious members: Louis Aragon, Brecht, Picasso, Paul Langevin, Pablo Neruda. The party made a point of keeping these members on the sidelines in order to confine their adherence to chance, mood, interest, or circumstance. But despite the superficial nature of these artists' adherence, the painting of Picasso (see *The Massacres of Korea*) and the poetry of Neruda and Aragon suffered because of it. Artistically, adherence could survive in a style of provocation. The embrace of ideology by superior minds came about through a random confluence of diverse nonideological passions. But as these passions came closer to the heart of the ideology, they faded. Sometimes, a residue of ineptitude was all that remained.

In the communist zone, leaders sometimes took it upon themselves to collect and publish the basic tenets of their ideology under their own names. Such was the case with Stalin and Mao. These basic outlines amount to a few pages containing the entire doctrine: no treatise was deemed superior to these manuals, which were sometimes described as "elementary" to make people believe that more scholarly ones also existed. Although these longer works were no more than expanded and diluted versions of the same, this did not prevent them from being imposed as objects of "study"—which means that their subjects were required to spend hundreds of hours reviewing and mindlessly repeating their lessons. In the Nazi zone, such compendia did not exist. All thinking was supposed to hinge on that of the leader, who presented himself as oracular and inspired. In analyzing the substance of Nazism, one finds a miserable blend of social Darwinism, eugenics, a vaguely Nietzschean hatred for Christianity, a religion of "resentment," and pathological anti-Semitism.

The Nazi or communist presents a clinical case for psychiatric examination. He seems imprisoned, cut off from reality, capable of arguing indefinitely in circles with his interlocutor, obsessed. Yet he is convinced he is rational. This is why psychiatrists have established a link between this state of chronic systematized delirium and such conditions as schizophrenia and paranoia. If one ventures further into the examination, it becomes clear that this characterization is metaphorical. The most obvious sign that ideological insanity is artificial is that it is reversible: when the pressure ceases and circumstances change, one gets out all at once, as if from a dream. But it is a waking dream—one that does not block motility and maintains a certain apparently rational coherence. Outside the affected area, which is the superior part of the mind in a healthy person—the part that articulates religion, philosophy, and the "governing ideas of reason," as Kant would say—the comprehensive functions seem intact but focused on and enslaved by the surreal object. When one wakes, one's mind is empty; one's life and knowledge must be entirely relearned. Germany, which for a century had been the Athens of Europe, woke up stupefied by twelve years of Nazism. And how to describe Russia, which was subjugated to this pedagogy of the absurd far more systematically for seventy years, and where intellectual foundations were less established and more fragile?

These artificial mental illnesses were also epidemic and contagious. They have been compared to a sudden outbreak of the plague or the flu. Formally, the Nazification of Germany in 1933 and the Chinese Cultural Revolution indeed developed like a contagious disease. But such comparisons probably have only metaphorical value while we await a better understanding of these psychological pandemics.

The backdrop of moral destruction is ineptitude. It is its condition. Natural and shared awareness can be distorted only if one's conception of the world, one's link to reality, has first been disrupted. Whether this blindness is an extenuating circumstance or an integral part of the evil, I will not debate here. In any case, it does not suspend moral judgment.

THE NAZI FALSIFICATION OF THE GOOD

When we attempt to examine closely all that was done to people at the six camps listed in the first chapter (see page 1), words do not suffice, concepts fail, imagination refuses to conceive, and memory refuses to retain. We are outside of the human realm here, as though standing before a negative transcendence. The idea of the demonic arises irresistibly.

What suggests the demonic is that these acts were carried out in the name of a good, under the guise of a moral code. The instrument of moral destruction is a falsification of the good that allows the criminal—to an extent impossible to describe—to sweep aside any sense that he is doing evil.

During the war, Heinrich Himmler delivered several speeches to high-ranking officers and section leaders of the SS.[1] His tone was always one of moral exhortation.

The following passage rises above the contingent circumstances of the era, above even the immediate interests of the Reich, to touch the universal:

> All that we do must be justified in relation to our ancestors. If we do not find this moral connection, which is the deepest and best connection because it is the most natural, we will never rise to the level necessary to defeat Christianity and to constitute this German Reich, which will be a blessing to the entire world. For thousands of years, it has been the duty of the blond race

to rule the world and always to bring it happiness and
civilization. (June 9, 1942)

The good, according to Nazism, consisted in restoring a
natural order that history had corrupted. The proper hierarchical
organization of races had been overturned by the harmful
influences of Christianity ("this plague, the worst sickness that has
affected us throughout our history"), democracy, the rule of gold,
Bolshevism, and the Jews. The German Reich was the apex of the
natural order, but it made room for the other Germanic peoples—
the Scandinavians, the Dutch, and the Flemish. Even the British
empire, "a worldwide empire created by the white race," could
be left intact. The French and Italians were next in the hierarchy.
Further down were the Slavs, who would be enslaved and reduced
in number: Himmler contemplated a "reduction" of thirty million.
The natural order, according to which the best, the most hardened,
the purest, and the most chivalrous rule, would also be restored
within the German society. The living examples of men of this
nature were the elite of the Waffen-SS. By the time Himmler made
this speech, the incurable and disabled—those alienated from the
German "race"—had already been secretly euthanized in hospitals
and asylums.

All of this would not take place, Himmler continued, without an
extremely hard fight. In his speeches, he constantly invoked heroism,
going beyond oneself, and a sense of the higher duty his listeners
owed towards the Reich, especially when it concerned carrying out
difficult orders. "We must tackle our ideological duties and answer
to destiny, no matter what the situation is; we must always stand
tall and never fall or falter, but be ever present until our life comes
to an end or our task is accomplished."

From a certain standpoint, then, the "Final Solution" was only a
technical problem, like delousing when there is a danger of typhus:
"Destroying lice is not a question of world view. It is a question
of cleanliness. . . . Soon there will be no more lice" (April 24,

1934). The metaphor of the insect that must be destroyed turns up regularly in the discourse of ideological extermination. Lenin had already used it. But Himmler, good leader that he was, said this to reassure and encourage his audience. He knew that it was not easy, that false scruples could arise. But to accomplish a certain type of task, "it is always necessary to be aware of the fact that we are caught up in a primitive, natural, original, and racial battle" (December 1, 1943). These four adjectives appropriately describe the Nazi ethic.

In an October 6, 1943, address, Himmler stated his view of the Final Solution:

> The phrase "the Jews must be exterminated" consists of few words; it is quickly said, gentlemen. But what it requires for those who carry it out is the hardest and most difficult thing in the world. Naturally, these are Jews, just Jews, of course; but think of all those—even friends of the Party—who have made the famous request to some department or to myself saying, "Of course, all Jews are swine, except Mr. So-and-so, who is a decent Jew and should not be harmed." I dare say that judging by the number of these requests and the number of these opinions in Germany, there were more decent Jews than existed nominally. . . . I insist that you simply listen to what I am saying here in this meeting and never speak of it. We were asked the following question: what are we to do with the women and children? I have come to a decision and have found an obvious solution for this matter also. I did not feel I had the right to exterminate the men—in other words, to kill them or have them killed—while allowing their children to grow up, children who would take revenge on our children and our descendants. It was necessary to make the serious decision to eliminate this people from the earth. For the organization that had to ac-

complish this task, it was the hardest thing it had done. I think I can say that this was accomplished without our men or our officers suffering because of it in their hearts or in their souls. Even so, this was a real danger. The path lies between the two possibilities: become too hardened, become heartless, and no longer respect human life; or else become too soft and lose one's mind to the point of having fits of hysterics—this path between Scylla and Charybdis is hopelessly narrow.

This virtuous golden mean that Himmler called for was occasionally attained: several great executioners were indeed loving fathers and sensitive husbands. The "task" had to be performed without the intervention of "selfish" motives—calmly, without nervous weakness. Indulging in drinking, raping a young girl, robbing the prisoners for one's profit, or stooping to pointless sadism showed a lack of discipline, disorder. Such actions marked a forgetting of Nazi idealism; they were blameworthy and had to be punished.

NAZI MORALITY DEMANDED that one follow the order that nature had established. But this natural order was not a matter of contemplation; it was deduced from ideology. With the pole of good represented by the "blond race" and that of evil by the "Jewish race," the cosmic battle was to end with the victory of one or the other.

But the whole thing was false. There are no "races" in the sense intended by the Nazis. The tall blond Aryan did not exist, even if there were Germans who were tall and blond. The Jew as represented by Nazism did not exist, because the racial representation that Nazism made of the Jews had only coincidental connections with the real identity of the people of the biblical covenant. The Nazi thought he saw nature, but nature was dissimulated by his interpretive grid.

Nor did he perceive the historical and military situation without distortion. Because of his "Nazism," Hitler went to war, and because of his same Nazism, he lost that war. The superiority of Stalin was that he was able to set his ideology aside long enough to prepare for victory. The Leninist ideology was "better" because it allowed for such pauses and authorized a political patience of which Nazism—impulsive and convulsive—was incapable.

The Nazi ethic manifested itself as a negation of the ethical tradition of all humanity. Only a few marginal thinkers had dared to advance some of its themes, but only as an aesthetic provocation. In fact, the kind of naturalism that it proposed—the superman, the subhuman, the will to power, nihilism, irrationalism—places it more in the domain of aesthetics. It is the artistic kitsch that intoxicates, the staging of Nuremberg, the colossal architecture à la Speer, the dark splendor of brute force. As a morality, the Nazi ethic cannot gain serious support in history. Its perversity easily becomes evident and it cannot be universalized.

The communist ethic, by contrast, can be universalized and its perversity is not readily evident. This explains why Nazi morality was less contagious than communist morality and why the moral destruction it engendered was more limited in scope. The "inferior" "subhuman" races saw an imminent deadly threat in this doctrine and could not be tempted. As for the German people themselves, to the extent that they followed Hitler, they did so out of nationalism rather than Nazism. Nationalism, a natural passion that has been particularly aroused during the last two centuries, supplied the Nazi regime's artificial constructs with energy and fuel, just as it supplied these for the communist regime. Although some members of the German elite had supported the chancellor's coming to power, the vulgar elitism of Hitler's troops had nothing to do with the old elite. Those who claimed to follow Nietzsche were caught in the trap like everyone else. As for the loyalty of the officer corps, it can be explained by military tradition, reinforced on occasion by a little Kantianism or Hegelianism. The soldiers obeyed simply as soldiers do.

That is why the theoretical crux of Nazism—the physical destruction of the Jewish people, then of other peoples in hierarchical order—was one of the best-kept secrets of the Reich. *Kristallnacht* was a test, an attempt to invite and rally the German people behind the great plan, but it was not a political success. Thus, Hitler decided to build the six major extermination camps outside the historical borders of Germany.

The moral damage of Nazism can be described in terms of concentric circles moving around the central core suggested by the passage quoted from Himmler. The central core consists of those who were converted to the fullness of Nazism. Few in number, these were the heart of the party, the heart of the Waffen-SS and the Gestapo. The practitioners of extermination were even fewer. They did not have to be numerous: the high level of German industrial and technological development made it possible to economize on manpower. The few hundred SS who controlled the death camps delegated the "manual" tasks to the victims themselves. The *Einsatzgruppen* were recruited without preliminary qualifications. It has been noted that, theoretically, members were allowed to leave these corps of murderers. But major troubles awaited them, the first of which was fighting on the Soviet front. The men of the *Einsatzgruppen* were—or became—monsters. Whether they were all converted to the Nazi ideology is still an open question. But in every population, it is easy to recruit as many torturers and murderers as are needed. The ideological veneer only made it easier for some to accept such a vocation; it allowed this vocation to flourish.

It has been noted that the Wehrmacht could not have been ignorant of the activity of the *Einsatzgruppen* that operated behind its lines. The destination of the convoys and liquidation of the ghettos did not leave much room for doubt; despite the no-man's-land surrounding the death camps, something eventually had to leak out. Hilberg writes that the secret was "a secret that everyone knew." That is probably true, but two points must be considered.

First, a secret that everyone knows is not the same thing as a proclaimed policy or a public fact. The Germans followed out of military and civic discipline, nationalism, fear, and the inability to devise or carry out an act of resistance. The secret—despite being out—released them from immediate moral responsibility, or at least allowed them to hedge, to look the other way, and to act as though it all did not exist. Under Nazism, German society still had remnants of law. The officer corps included a number of men who remained loyal to the canons of war and strove—with greater or lesser success—to maintain a certain honor. Because private property had not yet been abolished, civil society thrived. The film *Schindler's List* is built around the fact that a business owner was still able to recruit and house a Jewish workforce in Germany. From the first year of communism, such a thing was no longer conceivable in Russia.

Second, the contents of the secret were not believable for a normal mind. Much of Germany still lived in a natural society governed by a natural morality, and did not size up what was in store for it. This fact made it harder to believe that reality was being hidden from it, that the suspicions were well founded and the various clues obvious. Even Jews—who underwent expropriation, concentration, and deportation—did not always believe it when they arrived at the gas chambers.

Nazi pedagogy was practiced for only a few years. When Germany was occupied, Nazism disappeared immediately—at least in the Western Zone (in the East, it was put in part to new use). It disappeared, first, because it was tried and sentenced at all levels under German and international law. Another reason was that the majority of the population had not been deeply saturated with it. Finally, Nazism disappeared because even the Nazis, once awakened, did not clearly see the link between what they had been under the ideology's magic spell and what they were now that this spell had worn off. Eichmann's fundamental nature was that of a middle-class bureaucrat; he had been this before and would have become again had he not been captured and punished. He greeted this punishment passively, in keeping with his bland character. As Hannah Arendt rightly pointed out, the crimes Eichmann was accused of were incommensurable with the limited consciousness of this banal being.

THE COMMUNIST FALSIFICATION OF THE GOOD

Communism was moral. A moral imperative underlay the entire prehistory of Bolshevism (French and German socialism, Russian populism), and the victory of Bolshevism was celebrated as a victory of the good. Aesthetics did not take precedence over ethics. The Nazi considered himself an artist; the communist, a virtuous man.

The foundation of communism's morality lay in its interpretive system, one deduced from knowledge. Primitive nature, the system taught, was not the hierarchical, cruel, implacable nature in which the superior Nazi man rejoices, but resembled the goodness of nature according to Rousseau. Nature had been lost, but socialism would re-create it by lifting it to a higher level. There, man would be completely fulfilled. Trotsky claimed that such exemplars as Michelangelo and da Vinci would mark the base level of the new humanity. Communism democratized the superman.

Natural progress was regarded as historical progress, since historical and dialectical materialism unifies nature and history. Communism appropriated Progress, that great theme of the Enlightenment, in contrast with the theme of decadence that haunted Nazism; but in this case, dramatic progress included tremendous and unavoidable destruction. One recognizes here bits of Hegelian pantragism[2] and particularly the hardcore Darwinism of the struggle to survive applied to society. The "social relations of production" ("slavery," "feudalism," "capitalism") succeeded one another like the various reigns in the animal kingdom, as when the mammals took over from the reptiles. Such progressivism was a secret point of agreement between Nazism and communism: you don't cry over spilled milk; you can't make an omelette without breaking eggs; when you chop wood, the chips fly—all these expressions were familiar to Stalin. On both sides, history was the master. Nazism would restore the world in its beauty; communism, in its goodness.

The communist restoration depended on the human will enlightened by ideology. Even more clearly than Nazism, Leninism followed the gnostic blueprint of two antagonistic principles and three periods. In the beginning, there was the primitive commune; in the future, there would be communism; today, there was the period of the battle between the two principles. The forces that furthered "progress" were deemed good and those that hindered it were bad. The scientifically guaranteed ideology designated the bad principle. Not a biological entity in the sense of an inferior race, that principle was a social entity seen to grow like a cancer throughout society: it was property, capitalism, and the complex of mores, law, and culture summed up in the expression "the spirit of capitalism." Those who had understood the three periods and two principles, who were acquainted with the essence of the naturo-historical order, who knew both the direction of its evolution and the means to hasten it—these people came together and formed the party.

All means that would bring about the end as foreseen by the revolutionary were considered good. Since the process was as natural as it was historical, destruction of the old order would in itself bring about the new order. Bakunin's expression, summarizing what he had understood from Hegel, was the maxim of Bolshevism: the spirit of destruction is the same as the spirit of creation. In Bolshevism's prehistory, the *Narodnik* heroes were conscious of the moral revolution that followed from these ideas. Chernyshevsky, Nechayev, and Tkachyov developed a literature of "the new man," one Dostoyevsky satirized and whose metaphysical meaning he grasped. The new man appropriated the new morality of an absolute devotion to the ends. This new morality required one to drive out the remnants of the old morality, which "class enemies" advanced in order to perpetuate their rule. Lenin canonized communist ethics.

Trotsky wrote a pamphlet whose title says it all: *Their Morality and Ours*.

THEIR MORALITY AND OURS

What is amazing is that not everyone outside of this revolutionary milieu was aware of this moral rupture. In fact, communism used words from the old morality—justice, equality, liberty, etc.—to describe the new one. It is true that the world communism planned to destroy was full of injustice and oppression. Virtuous men had to acknowledge that the communists denounced these evils with extreme vigor. Everyone agreed that distributive justice was not upheld. The good man, guided by a sense of justice, attempted to promote a better distribution of wealth. The communist, by contrast, saw the idea of justice consisting not in a "fair" distribution of wealth, but in the establishment of socialism and suppression of private property—this consequently voided all standards of fairness, fairness itself, and ultimately the right of individuals. The communist commitment to creating an awareness of inequality did not aim to call attention to a defect of law, but to elicit desire for a society in which regulation would not be a matter of law. Similarly, the communist idea of liberty aimed to arouse the awareness of oppression in circumstances in which the individual—a victim of capitalist alienation—believed he was free. Finally, all the words that were used to express modalities of the good—justice, liberty, humanity, goodness, generosity, achievement—were directed towards a single goal that encompassed and fulfilled them all: communism. In the communist perspective, these words were no more than homonyms of the old words.

Yet some simple criteria should have cleared up this confusion. By natural or common morality I mean the morality referred to by the sages not only of antiquity, but also of China, India, and Africa. In the world of the Bible, this morality is summed up in the second table of the commandments of Moses. Communist ethics opposed common morality head-on, and very consciously. The communist ethic sought to destroy ownership—and the laws and liberty connected to it—and to reform the order of the family. By permitting itself all manner of lies and violence in order to overcome the old order and call forth the new, it openly and fundamentally infringed upon the fifth commandment ("Honor thy father and thy mother"), the sixth ("Thou shalt not kill"), the seventh ("Thou shalt not commit adultery"), the eighth ("Thou shalt not steal"), the ninth ("Thou shalt not bear false witness against thy neighbor"), and the tenth ("Thou shalt not covet that which is thy neighbor's"). It is not at all necessary to believe in biblical revelation to accept the spirit of these precepts, which are found throughout the earth. The majority of mankind honors the idea that certain behaviors are true and good because they correspond to what we know of the structure of the universe. Communism, which conceived of another universe, derived its morality from that. This is why communism challenged not only the precepts, but also their foundation: the natural world. Although I said previously that communist morality was based on nature and history, this in fact was not true: it was based on a super-nature that never existed and on a history devoid of truth.

In *Democracy and Totalitarianism*, Raymond Aron argues that

> the Soviet regime came from a revolutionary will inspired by a humanitarian ideal. The goal was to create the most humane regime history had ever known, the first regime in which everyone could achieve humanity, where classes would disappear, and where the homogeneity of society would allow for the mutual recognition of citizens. But this movement aiming at an absolute goal did not shrink from any means: according to the doctrine, only violence could create this absolutely good society, and the proletariat was involved in a ruthless war with capitalism. From this combination of a

> sublime goal and ruthless methods, the different phases
> of the Soviet regime arose.[3]

These lines reflect, with all possible clarity, the ambiguity and illusion of communism. What it labeled the human and the humanitarian was really the superhuman and superhumanitarian promised by the ideology. The human and the humanitarian had neither rights nor a future. Classes were not reconciled; they were to disappear. Society did not become homogeneous; its autonomy and its proper dynamic were destroyed. The war against capitalism was waged not by the proletariat, but by the ideological sect that spoke and acted in its name. Finally, capitalism existed solely in opposition to a socialism that existed nowhere but in the ideology; consequently, the concept of capitalism was inadequate to describing the reality that had to be brought down. The goal was not sublime: it took on the colors of sublimity. The means, which was killing, became the only possible end.

After drawing a long and admirable parallel between Nazism and communism, Raymond Aron writes:

> I will maintain to the end that the difference between
> these two phenomena is an essential one, whatever the
> similarities may be. The difference is essential because
> of the idea that drives each of the two enterprises. In
> one case, the final outcome is the labor camp; in the
> other, it is the gas chamber. In the one case, there is at
> work a will to build a new regime—and perhaps a new
> man—using any means; in the other, what is at work is
> a properly demonic will to destroy a pseudo-race.[4]

I, too, acknowledge the difference, but on the basis of arguments I will expound below. I am not convinced by those Aron presents here. Nazism also planned for a new regime and a new man using any means. It is impossible to decide which is more demonic:

destroying a pseudo-race and then successively destroying the other pseudo-races—including the "superior" one—because they are all polluted, or destroying a pseudo-class and then successively destroying the others, which are all contaminated by the spirit of capitalism.

Raymond Aron concludes:

> If I had to summarize the meaning of each of the two enterprises, I think these are the phrases I would suggest: concerning the Soviet enterprise, I would quote the trite expression "he who wants to play the angel plays the beast." Concerning the Hitlerian enterprise, I would say: "it would be wrong for man to set a goal to become like a beast of prey: he pulls it off too well."

Is it better to be a beast that plays the angel or a man that plays the beast—given that both are beasts "of prey"? This is indeterminable. In the first case, the degree of the lie is stronger and the appeal is greater. The communist falsification of the good went deeper, since the crime more closely resembled the good than the naked crime of the Nazi. This trait allowed communism to expand more widely and to work on hearts that would have turned away from an SS calling. Making good men bad is perhaps more demonic than making men who are already bad worse. Raymond Aron's argument boils down to a difference of intentions: the Nazi intention contradicted the universal idea of the good, whereas the communist intention perverted it, because it had the appearance of good. But it tricked many more inattentive souls to go along with it as a result. Because the communist project was unattainable, we are left to judge only the means; but because these means were incapable of attaining their end, they became the real end. The lie overlaid the crime, making it all the more tempting and dangerous.

Leninist communism is more tempting because it appropriates an ancient ideal—albeit by removing it from its heritage. At the time they became adherents, many were unable to discern the corruption brought about by Leninism. Some people remained communists for a long time, even all their lives, without realizing it. The confusion of the old (common) morality with the new morality was never completely dispelled. Thus, a number of "decent people," those whose moral decay was delayed, remained in communist parties. Their presence counts in favor of granting collective amnesty. The former communist has been more easily forgiven than the former Nazi, who was suspected of having consciously broken with common morality from the time of his joining.

Communism is more dangerous because its education is insidious and gradual; it disguises the evil acts it causes as good acts. It is also more dangerous because it is unpredictable to its future victims: anyone can potentially assume enemy status from one moment to the next. Nazism designated its enemies in advance. True, it endowed them with a fantastical nature bearing no relation to reality. But behind the subhuman, there was a real Jew, behind the despicable Slav, a Pole or a Ukrainian in flesh and blood. Those who were neither Jewish nor Slavic got a reprieve. The same universalism that had represented the great superiority of communism over Nazi exclusiveness before the communists' seizure of power became a universal threat once the communists were in power. Capitalism, as the word was employed, existed only ideologically. No category of humanity was spared the curse it bore: whether the "middle" and "poor" peasantry, the intelligentsia, the "proletariat," or the party itself. Because anyone could be contaminated by the spirit of capitalism, no one was safe from suspicion.

WITH A CERTAIN realism, Nazi leaders promised blood and tears and anticipated a fight to the death to restore humanity to its proper racial order. Lenin, on the contrary, thought that the time was right and the eschatology would be realized as soon as "capitalism" was overthrown. The revolution was going to sweep over the entire world. Once the expropriators were expropriated, socialist administration would spontaneously move into position. But nothing happened on the day following November 7, 1917: the curtain rose on an empty stage. Where did the proletariat, the poor and middle peasantry, and proletarian internationalism all go? Lenin was alone with his party (and a few Red Guards) in a hostile or indifferent world.

Still, because Marxism-Leninism was "scientific," experience had to validate the theory. With capitalism overthrown, socialism had to take over. But since this did not seem to be happening, socialism had to be constructed along the lines indicated by the theory and each step had to be verified to ensure that the result would be true to the prediction. Piece by piece, a universe of lies was constructed to replace the truth. An atmosphere of widespread lies thickened as the facts increasingly diverged from the words that were supposed to describe them. The good asserted itself frenetically in order to deny the reality of evil.

This, mainly, is how moral destruction occurs in the communist regime. As in the Nazi regime, it expands in concentric circles around an initial core.

At the center lies the party, and in the party, its ruling circle. When the party first comes to power, it is still completely in the grip of ideology. This is the time when it makes every effort to eliminate "the class enemy." Its moral conscience completely poisoned, the party destroys entire categories of human beings in the name of its utopia. A retrospective view shows that, in the cases of Russia, Korea, China, Romania, Poland, and Cambodia, the initial slaughters were some of the most significant in the history of these regimes—their toll was something on the order of 10 percent or more of the population.

When it turns out that the utopian dream is still not being realized, that the propitiatory decimation has been useless, there is a gradual shift from seeking a utopia to merely preserving power. Given that the objective enemy has already been exterminated, vigilance is now required. It must not be allowed to regroup, let alone to rise up in the very ranks of the party. A second terror arises, a time that seems absurd because it corresponds to no social and political resistance, but aims at a total control of all human beings and all thought. Fear then becomes universal: it spreads within the party itself, and every member feels threatened by it. Everyone denounces everyone else, and all are caught in a chain reaction of betrayal.

Next comes the third stage. Taking precautions against a permanent purge, the party now contents itself with a routine management of power and security. It no longer believes in the ideology, but continues to speak its language. The party sees that this language, which it knows to be a lie, is the only one spoken because it is the mark of the party's domination. The party accumulates privileges and advantages; it becomes a caste. Corruption within the party becomes widespread. The people compare its members no longer to wolves, but to swine.

The periphery is composed of the rest of the population, which is immediately summoned and mobilized for the building of socialism. The entire periphery is threatened, fed lies, and solicited to participate in the crime.

The first step of the mobilization process is to seal off the periphery. As one of its first acts, every communist government closes its borders. Until 1939, the Nazis authorized departures in exchange for ransom—this served the "purity" of Germany. But the communists never did this: they needed their borders completely sealed off to protect the secret of their slaughter, of their failure. But they especially needed such isolation because the country was supposed to become an extensive school where all would receive the education that would eradicate the spirit of capitalism and instill the socialist spirit in its place.

The second step is to control information. The population must not know what goes on beyond the socialist camp. It must not know what goes on inside either. Indeed, it must not know its past or its present—only its radiant future.

The third step is to replace reality with a pseudo-reality. To this end, a whole corps specializes in the production of false journalists, false historians, a false literature, and a false art that pretends to reflect a fictitious reality as in a photograph. A false economy produces imaginary statistics. Sometimes, the need for cosmetic retouches led to Nazi-style measures. In the USSR, for example, disabled ex-servicemen and workers were removed from the public eye and taken to remote asylums where they could no longer spoil the picture. It has been reported that, in Korea, a decision has been made that the dwarf "race" must disappear; thus, dwarves are deported and prevented from procreating. Millions are involved in the construction of this immense stage production. What is its purpose? To prove that socialism is not only possible, but under construction, that it is growing stronger—or, better, that it has already been realized. There is a new, free, self-regulating society where "new human beings" think and act spontaneously within this fictitious reality. The strongest tool fabricated by this power is a new language in which existing words take on a meaning that differs from the common usage. The diction and special vocabulary of this new language endow it with the quality of a liturgical language; it denotes the transcendence of socialism and indicates the omnipotence of the party. Its popular use is the obvious sign of the people's servitude.

At first, a significant portion of the population welcomes the teaching of the lie in good faith. It enters into the new morality, taking along its old moral heritage. These people love the leaders who promise them happiness and they believe that they are happy. They think that they are living in a just order. Hating the enemies of socialism, they denounce them and approve of having them robbed and killed. They join in their extermination and lend their strength to the endeavor. Inadvertently, they take part in the crime. Along the way, ignorance, misinformation, and faulty reasoning numb their faculties and they lose their intellectual and moral bearings. When their sense of justice is offended, their inability to distinguish communism from the common moral ideal causes them to attribute the offense to the external enemy. Until the collapse of communism, people who were mistreated by the police or by militants in Russia commonly called them "fascists." It did not occur to them to call them by their true name: communists.

But life on this socialist stage—instead of becoming "more cheerful and happier," as Stalin said in the middle of the Great Purge—became grimmer, more dismal. Fear was everywhere and people had to fight to survive. The moral degradation that had been subconscious to that point now crept into consciousness. The socialist people, who had committed evil believing they were doing good, now knew what they were doing. They denounced, stole, and degraded themselves; they became evil and cowardly and they were ashamed. The communist regime did not hide its crimes as Nazism did; it proclaimed them and invited the population to join in. Each condemnation was followed by a meeting at which the accused was publicly cursed by his friends, his wife, his children. These yielded to the ceremony out of fear or out of self-interest. The enthusiastic Stakhanovite of an earlier era—if he had ever existed as anything but a prop—revealed himself to be a lazy, servile, idiotic *Homo sovieticus*. The women came to loathe the men and the children their parents—even though they sensed that they, in turn, were becoming like them.

The last stage is described for us by the writers of the end of Sovietism: Erofeev and Zinoviev. The most widespread feelings were despair and self-disgust. What remained was to take advantage of the specific pleasures this regime procured: irresponsibility, idleness, and vegetative passivity. One no longer made the effort to practice double-thought; one attempted simply to stop thinking entirely. One withdrew. As with the drunkard, tearful sentimentality and self-pity were a way to call others to witness one's degradation. In Zinoviev's "ratorium" one was still involved in the Hobbesian struggle of all against all, but with very little energy. Zinoviev considered *Homo sovieticus* to be the product of an irreversible mutation of the species—fortunately, he was probably wrong.

There was no safe haven where one could escape the teaching of the lie. The social structures of the old society had been destroyed along with private property, and had been replaced by new ones that were at once schools and places of surveillance: the *kolkhoz*, the Chinese popular commune for the peasant, the "trade union" for the worker, the "unions" for writers and artists. The history of these regimes can be described as a continuous race for universal control. From the standpoint of the subjects, it was a frantic race for places of refuge, or at the very least, for places to hide. And there were always places of refuge. In Russia, a few families of the old intelligentsia were able to preserve their traditions—an Andrei Sakharov emerged from this class. In the universities, there were more or less untroubled chairs of Assyriology or Greek philology, and in the subservient churches there were pockets of fresh air. At the end of the regime, small groups of young people could be found in Moscow. Having recovered their moral and intellectual lives, these people chose to live by their wits, not taking on any work or seeking any position, and minimized their contact with the external Soviet world. In this way, they were able to hold on until the very end.

In the Soviet empire, the communist zeal to reeducate stopped at the gate of the camp. For the Nazis, there was no need to convert subhumans, and the Bolsheviks practically abandoned the idea of converting prisoners. Solzhenitsyn could therefore state that the camp, in spite of its horrors, was a place of intellectual freedom and fresh spiritual air. Asian communism, on the contrary, made the camp the place where teaching was practiced in the most obsessive and cruel way. Authorities noted the progress of the prisoners. No one but the dead or the reeducated ever left.

ASSESSMENT

Within the limits imposed by the historical perspective adopted here, let us attempt a comparative assessment of the moral destruction wrought by Nazism and communism in the twentieth century.

By moral destruction, I do not mean the breakdown of mores in the sense of the age-old grumbling of the elderly as they examine the mores of the youth. Nor do I wish to pass judgment on this century compared to others. There is no philosophical reason to think that man was either more or less virtuous during this period. Still, communism and Nazism set out to change something more fundamental than mores—that is, the very rule of morality, of our sense of good and evil. And in this, they committed acts unknown in prior human experience.

Even though the Nazis carried crime to a level of intensity perhaps unequaled by communism, one must nevertheless affirm that communism brought about a more widespread and deeper moral destruction. There are two reasons for this.

First, the obligation to internalize the new moral code extended to the entire population subjected to reeducation. Accounts tell us that this compulsory internalization was the most unbearable part of communist oppression: all the rest—the absence of political and civil liberties, police surveillance, physical repression, and fear itself—was nothing compared to this mutilating pedagogy. Having driven its victims mad because it contradicted what was obvious to the senses and understanding, it did so all the more because the whole range of "measures" and "organs" were ultimately subjected to this indoctrination. Communism, unlike Nazism, had the time to pursue its pedagogy, and it did so to the full extent. Its collapse or retreat has left behind a disfigured humanity. The poisoning of souls is more difficult to purge from the former communist bloc than it was from Germany. The latter nation, stricken with a temporary insanity, awoke from its nightmare ready for work, self-examination, and a purifying repentance.

Next, the moral destruction of communism was worse because the confusion between common morality and communist morality remains deep rooted. With the latter hiding behind the former, it is parasitical and polluting, using common morality to spread its contagion. Here is a recent example: in the discussions that followed the publication of *The Black Book of Communism*, an editorial writer at the French communist newspaper *L'Humanité* announced on television that 85 million deaths did not in any way tarnish the communist ideal. They represented only a very unfortunate deviation. After Auschwitz, he continued, one can no longer be a Nazi, but one can remain a communist after the Soviet camps. This man, who spoke in good conscience, did not realize at all that he had just articulated his own most fatal condemnation. He could not see that the communist idea had so perverted the principles of reality and morality that it could indeed outlive 85 million corpses, whereas the Nazi idea had succumbed under its dead. He thought he had spoken as a great and decent man, idealistic and uncompromising, without realizing that he had uttered a monstrosity. Communism is more perverse than Nazism because it does not ask man consciously to take the moral step of the criminal, and because it uses the spirit of justice and goodness that abounds throughout the earth to spread evil over all the earth. Each communist experience begins anew in innocence.

CHAPTER 3
THE DESTRUCTION OF POLITICAL LIFE

I HAVE DISCUSSED the destruction of human beings in terms of both their physical nature and their moral nature as rational beings capable of discerning between good and evil. It is still necessary to consider the destruction of their political nature—that is, of their ability to form family ties, social ties, and organized relationships between the governing and the governed for the sake of forming a political community, a state.

THE POLITICS OF THE DESTRUCTION OF POLITICAL LIFE

Before seizing power, and in order to seize it, communist and Nazi parties used all political means available. They became involved in the political game, even though they placed themselves—according to their own criteria and internal discipline—outside the political arena. For example, when the Bolshevik Party demanded land for the peasants and an immediate peace, it was not satisfied simply by the success of these two demands. It sought to use that success to bring the peasants and the soldiers over to its side in order to launch the revolutionary process. Once the revolution ended, the land was expropriated from the peasants and war was actively prepared for—without the party having seen the slightest contradiction in this. None of its actions came to an end with the attainment of its stated objective. Each action was always part of an unlimited movement and was undertaken only in order to prepare for a further act extending beyond the declared limit.

Once in power, the Communist Party aimed its policies more than ever at the destruction of political life. Organic forms of social life were to be eliminated—whether classes, interest groups, constituent bodies, or the family (consistently, the family resisted elimination, although its bonds were eroded and grew weaker). Now deprived of all rights of association, spontaneous aggregation, and representation, human beings were reduced to the status of atoms and pushed into a new form of organization. Because this organization was modeled on the one that was supposed to come into existence under socialism, it adopted the corresponding names: Soviets, unions, communes. Since socialism existed only virtually, these structures actually existed only as constraints. It was strictly political expediency that preferred new administrative structures to express this virtual socialism; old names were retained only in order to give the impression that the old world still existed to some extent. If the old terms could still be "put to political use," structures were called trade unions, academies, parliaments, or cooperatives. How many Western parliamentary or municipal delegations were thus deceived? How many thought they were being welcomed by members of parliament and local dignitaries rather than by party officials who had simply assumed these names?

Broadly speaking, the Nazi Party imitated the communist destruction of political life. It too seized power by concealing its real objectives and deceiving its temporary allies among the conservative right in order to crush them. It too created a new administrative class and recruited youths and the "masses" to join it. Because its design did not require an immediate destruction of the old orders, it contented itself with neutralizing and subjugating them. Entrepreneurship, a market, a judiciary, and traditional government offices thus remained under Nazism. Still guided by the old rules, these institutions continued to function and were not replaced. Then came the war, which increased and accelerated the Nazi grip. As for what would have happened had the Nazis won the war, it is impossible to guess.

THE RESIDUE OF POLITICAL LIFE

The Führer Principle was an essential part of the Nazis' understanding of a return to nature. The social network was to be organized around a hierarchy of loyal leaders that were devoted to the Reich and bound by an oath. This hierarchy was to reach up to the supreme leader. Exaltation of this leader was consistent with the spirit of the system.

The Communist Party was also hierarchical. Theoretically, it rested on a democratic and electoral basis. But in fact, from the time of its founding, the inner circle of Lenin's party dictated to those at the "base" who should be elected. Democratic election simply became an opportunity to test the omnipotence of the center. The gnostic conscience, the founding scientific knowledge of the party, was theoretically concentrated in the ruling body. From this point on, it radiated towards the "base," which, by sending its power towards the "center," demonstrated the progress it had made in assimilating the doctrine and "party line." Thus, a leader cult developed—one that began at the time of Lenin and reached its peak under Stalin. The cult lived on into the Brezhnev era, but the hollowness of the idol had become apparent. Because the leadership cult was contrary to communist doctrine, Trotskyite purists denounced it indignantly. Yet it represented a resurgence of real human nature in a system based on an unreal supernature. To venerate one's fellow man accords more with human nature than to worship an abstract body of doctrine that is obviously false.

Thus, a residue of political life remained only to the degree that communist and Nazi power was incarnated in real people. Political life was reduced to Montesquieu's vision of the Ottoman or Persian seraglio: to a mixture of hatred and scheming among people and clans that were precariously united for the purpose of gaining personal power. Trotsky, Bukharin, Zinoviev, and Stalin all aimed at the same socialist goal, but one of them *had* to be number one. Thus, a succession of betrayals and murders occurred behind closed doors.

UTOPIA

The inexhaustible, cunning, and occasionally frantic activity of the core leadership cannot be described as political, because it was subjugated to the creation of a utopia.

Both Nazi and communist regimes referred to a mythical past upon which an imaginary future would be modeled. For the Nazis, the past held the Aryans, the best people according to nature: tomorrow the Germans would rule again, and over them, the most pure. Communism insisted less on restoring the past—the primitive commune—than on reproducing it at a "higher level." Thus, it made greater use of the old notion of progress that had been inherited from the Enlightenment and dramatized by Romanticism. The Marxist idea, according to Raymond Aron, sought to go from Rousseau to Rousseau by way of Saint-Simon—in other words, by means of technical and industrial progress. Hitlerism was voluntaristic: only the demiurgic work of the will was capable of restoring the biological equilibrium of the good jungle. Leninism, by contrast, relied on historical inevitability to give birth to a modern Arcadia. Characterized by electricity and abundance, it would mark an *Aufhebung* of the original Arcadia. But historical inevitability, of course, had also produced the party as the midwife of this new birth. Although voluntarism was also necessary here, it was extolled and denied at the same time: the party was said to embody only the conscience of necessity fused (and here Lenin invokes Spinoza!) with freedom.

Wedged between a mythical past and an ideal future, the present had no value. Thus, politics also had no value, to the extent that the art of politics consists of equipping a people for the present by carefully managing the heritage of a past that is considered precious and living. Using short-term predictions as its guide, the political art permits no pretensions about the long term. As such, the political art meant nothing to Nazi or communist leaders. The recent past was the enemy; the present did not count. And everything was subjected to an eschatological future, to the final end.

THE UNLIMITED GOALS OF NAZISM

Was Nazism's field of expansion and activity limited or was it by nature unlimited? This question must be asked. The policy of appeasement adopted by Neville Chamberlain (and to a certain extent the policy of sharing adopted by Stalin in 1940) assumed that Hitler could be satisfied with what he had already obtained. Had he not shredded the Treaty of Versailles and acquired enough "land to the East" to keep himself busy for a few years? Having reorganized Germany, he had also eliminated the unfit and the Jews—the inferior people. Yet he still felt the need to go further. In order to conquer Poland, he ran the risk of waging war in the West. Next, he took the risk of provoking a world war. Although he probably did not see where his plan was leading him, he accepted the consequences, as if led by a higher destiny, and he continually restarted the game. The only partner with whom he could have managed an enduring partitioning of the world was Stalin. For his part, Stalin attributed to Hitler a rationality analogous to his own; aware of the natural bond between the two regimes, he had every reason to trust their alliance. But Hitler betrayed him, and Stalin never understood why. Then, with incomprehensible fickleness, Hitler declared war on the United States. From then on, he was involved in a venture that would either grant him victory and a world empire or defeat and the total ruin of Germany.

In this war, Nazism discovered its vocation to exterminate all mankind one segment at a time. The more the world resisted it, the more the Aryan-Jewish polarity became evident. The Jew appeared as the sign of resistance to the fulfillment of the great plan. Judaism merged with Bolshevism, which became Judeo-Bolshevism; capitalism, likewise, became Judeo-capitalism. The Jew had thus corrupted the entire world, polluted everything, "Judaicized" everything. All of humanity had to be purified and thus exterminated. As Sebastien Haffner has demonstrated, Hitler's final effort was to orchestrate the inevitable defeat such that it would lead to the destruction of Germany.[1] According to this interpretation, the goal of the Battle of the Bulge was to slow the American advance in order to hand the country over to the Soviets:

> The orders of annihilation given by Hitler on March 18 and 19, 1945, were not aimed at a heroic final struggle, as was still the case in the fall of 1944. For such a struggle, it would have been useless to put hundreds of thousands of Germans on the path of death, towards the interior of the country, or simultaneously to have destroyed all that could be of use to the humblest survivors. The sole purpose of Hitler's last genocide, now turned on Germany, was to punish the Germans for their refusal to volunteer for a heroic final struggle, to play the role that Hitler had assigned them. In Hitler's view, this constituted and had always constituted a crime punishable by death. A people who did not take on the role it had been given had to die.

The Nazi command structure, based on the decision of the leader, lent the regime an air of unpredictability. Theoretically, it was conceivable that Hitler would have joined with England in 1939 and been content with what Stalin had granted him. But this was not to be: he refused to build "Nazism in a single country." Likewise, the Nazi Party and SS empire did not need to replace the normal leaders of German industry, which had shown a capacity for strict obedience. Yet they still seized the controls, thereby introducing a Soviet-style chaos that was very damaging to the Reich's war effort.

The restructuring of the world might have been achieved in successive steps, the concomitant destruction occurring in an orderly fashion. The Nazis had indeed employed "salami tactics" (an expression attributed to Rakosi), in that each "race" that was at first spared saw its turn coming next. But the movement spun out of control very quickly and turned into a widespread massacre. The Nazis could not promise Ukrainians independence as Stalin would have done, prepared to settle his scores with the Ukrainians after the victory. No, the Nazis had to start exterminating them immediately. This, of course, set the Ukrainians against them. The doctrine's aestheticism was probably the cause of this ruinous "all-at-once" strategy. Hitler saw himself as an artist, and as such, was marked by the romantic aesthetic of genius. Kant wrote that

> the genius cannot scientifically explain how he achieves his work, but by his nature he sets the standard. And in this way, the author of a work that is a product of genius does not himself know how the ideas came to him. It lies in his power neither methodically to form similar ideas at will, nor to communicate to others the precepts that place him in a position to produce similar works.[2]

For this reason, Hitler did not really know what he was doing; nor did he know where his inspiration and decisions came from. He saw himself as a Promethean demiurge, and his intoxication spread in part to his people. He believed that he was the inspired vehicle of the *Volksgeist* (the spirit of the people), and that his orders—which were at first sensible, then insane—came from a higher source. Hence the Nazis' impatience and haste, which Stalin could not understand. Hence the irrationality of the conduct of the war. A number of decisions his excellent generals desired might not have won the war, but they might at least have stopped it at a draw—if only, that is, the war had had limited goals. But Hitler, in his wild Wagnerism, rejected all such limits and the war was lost.

THE UNLIMITED GOALS OF COMMUNISM

The communist project was total from the outset. Externally, it aimed at world revolution; internally, it sought a radical transformation of society, culture, even the human being. But it authorized the use of rational means in order to obtain these goals foreign to reason. During the war, Lenin was a wild dreamer; he imposed on the reality of the world such abstract entities as capitalism, imperialism, opportunism, leftism, and many other "isms" that explained everything in his view. He applied those "isms" to Switzerland as he did to Germany and Russia. But when he returned home to Russia, there was nothing so rigorously "political," in the Machiavellian sense, as his conquest of power.

The seizing of power by a communist party is prepared by a purely political struggle within a normal political society. During this phase, the party practices the same tactics it implements after its victory. The "salami tactics," for example, call for forming alliances with noncommunist political forces in order to force the ally to participate in the elimination of adversaries. The first to go is the "extreme right," with the help of all of the left, then the moderate section of this left. This progresses until the last "slice" must submit and "fuse" or be eliminated in turn. A professionalism that includes cunning, patience, and rationality regarding the desired goal is the hallmark of Leninism's superiority. But destruction is necessarily the endgame. Construction is impossible because the goal is insane.

Having become a kind of dictator without realizing it, Lenin continued imposing his imaginary categories on the most precarious situations and he made his decisions accordingly. Communist practice does not follow an aesthetic inspiration, but aspires to proceed at every moment from "scientific" deliberation. False science borrows the demonstrative appearance and logical procedure of true science. But this only makes the enterprise crazier, the decisions more implacable, and any correction of course more difficult. Because false science is not empirical, it fails to accept the results of its experiments.

The destruction gradually spreads and becomes a general one, likening itself (to borrow Bakunin's expression once again) to the will of creation. In Russia, this destruction proceeded according to the following steps.

First, there was destruction of the political adversary, of government agencies and the old administration. This was done in the blink of an eye in the days following the October putsch. Next came the destruction of all real or potential sources of social resistance, of such organized bodies as parties, the army, trade unions, and cooperatives, and of such cultural bodies as universities, schools, the academy, the church, publishing houses, and the press. But as the party realized that socialism still did not exist as a free and self-regulating society, it regarded coercion to be more necessary than ever to make it happen. The doctrine thus envisaged a world in which only two realities—socialism and capitalism—existed. Reality itself was confused with capitalism, which meant that all reality had to be destroyed. This was the third step: destruction of the village, the family, the remnants of bourgeois education, and the Russian language. Control had to extend over each individual. Each was rendered solitary and helpless by the destruction of the framework of his life; each had to be driven into a new framework where he would be reeducated and reconditioned. This was thought to be the way to eliminate hidden enemies.

The failure of the internal construction of socialism was seen to stem from a hostile external environment. Whatever the form of this hostile specter—bourgeois democracy, social democracy, or fascism—its mere existence was a threat. The fourth step then followed: Bolshevik-style organizations or communist parties had to be created in each country. A central body, the Comintern, would coordinate them and make them conform to the central model. When, with the help of circumstances, communism was able to expand, the newly annexed areas of the "socialist camp" experienced similar stages of destruction.

Throughout the entire camp, the party (through the voice of Stalin) insisted that "capitalism [was] stronger than ever." Capitalism was seen to have seeped in and infected the party, which had itself lost its vigor. It therefore remained to the party leader—and to him alone—to destroy the party (the fifth step) and re-create another one from its ashes. This dangerous operation called for an increase in the leader's charisma, thus making him more like the Nazi führer. Once Stalin was able to concentrate the spirit of history in his person—as Hitler had done with the spirit of the "race"—he could allow himself, in splendid isolation and a "direct" relationship with the masses, to eliminate their collective oppressor. Stalin did this once. In doing so, he imitated Hitler and his "Night of the Long Knives." He had been preparing to do it a second time (and maybe to deport all Jews) when death overtook him. Mao Tse-tung did it twice: during the period of the "Great Leap Forward" and then, even more distinctly, during the Cultural Revolution.

DISINTEGRATION AND SELF-DESTRUCTION

Taken to its limit, the pure logic of the two systems entailed an extermination of the entire population of the world. But this logic was not applied. Indeed, it cannot be applied to its logical conclusion.

The principle of communism was to subordinate everything to the seizing and preserving of power, because it was the responsibility of power to carry out the project. In order to preserve this power, the elements necessary for its subsistence had to be spared.

At times, the destruction caused damage such that the power of the party risked facing not a widespread revolt—this it knew how to avoid—but the disappearance of the human material over which its power was exercised. This is what happened after "war communism." Russia was dissolving, being liquefied, when Lenin declared that the New Economic Policy was on hold.

As long as the revolution was not victorious worldwide, the outside world, even if what was left was a minute island, constituted a deadly threat. Its mere existence risked bursting the bubble of the socialist fiction, and it mattered little whether it was truly hostile— as it was, all things considered, only once under Hitler—or whether it wanted only tranquility and the status quo, as the West did after the defeat of Nazism. In order to keep the real world at a distance, and possibly to destroy it, the party had to have real power at its disposal. But this power could be derived only from the reality it controlled. The party needed a minimally effective economy to provide for the population, and a minimum of technology and industry to equip the army. Therefore producers, technicians, and experts remained. The party could not move all that existed to the other side of the mirror. If it did, it too would be swallowed up by the oblivion it had produced.

Finally, the last step—destruction of the party itself—clashed with vital survival instincts. After the great purges of Stalin and Mao, the party took precautions and implemented conservative measures. Communists no longer killed other communists; they merely disgraced each other.

This is what triggered the decline of the system in Russia. The party aged because the preservation of power eventually became identified with the preservation of jobs and positions. Tactics perfected at critical moments were no longer used. Brezhnev slowly rotted in the top position. The party became corrupt: no longer dedicated to the objectives of communism, it sought simply to enjoy power and wealth. It left unreality and entered into the reality that had been devastated by its care. Here it found (albeit in abundance) only crude and unadorned goods: vodka, *dachas*, and large automobiles. As for the people, they wallowed in that portion of reality that had always been allotted them and managed as they could. And they increasingly lost interest in a regime that no longer offered them even the consolation of the fall of the mighty and the opportunity to take their places. The widespread deterioration reached a climax when a random flick of the finger made the house of cards collapse. In an event that could have happened much sooner or much later, we finally saw the postcommunist landscape as it was: populated by Mafioso and pseudo-bums that no longer had the energy even to remember.

In China, survivors of the Maoist purges took a different path. The needs of pure power, combined with a concern to develop the power of China and a dead communism, were infused with a living nationalism. As contemporaries of the decline of Sovietism, Chinese communists regretted having followed a bad development model at a time when other parts of the Chinese world had successfully followed a better one. Hence the ambiguous nature of present-day China: it is developing at full pace, but the party is not loosening its hold. No one knows if it is still a communist regime. Circumstances are such that only one pure communist regime remains: North Korea. Up to the present, it is one that has preferred the logic of self-annihilation.

NO ONE KNOWS how Nazism would have evolved. It never reached its summit and was overthrown at the beginning of its expansion. The order of its destructions was not the same as the order followed by those of Soviet communism. It turned outward before completing the transformation of German society. The USSR preferred organized subversion and a programmed repulsion of the "external" enemy. The Red Army would come only to seal the political victory. Nazism, for its part, immediately resorted to war. War tremendously accelerated the Nazi program. But in doing so, it also provoked a worldwide resistance that was quickly victorious.

Nazism's element of randomness leads one to think that Hitler could have achieved a peace of compromise that would have left him with a vast and stable territory. In that case, after Hitler's death, the regime would have worn down in a process similar to the one that characterized the Leninist regime. Leszek Kolakowski has written an apologue on this question. He imagined a *New York Times* article written in the 1980s, in the style of the articles the *Times* had been publishing at that time on Brezhnev's USSR. The journalist was very pleased with the softening of political mores and the universally noted progress of Nazism with a human face. The brutalities of yesteryear were indeed appalling, particularly the very severe fate reserved for the Jews. But these belonged to a past that was already rather distant, and should not cause people to forget the brilliant achievements that must be credited to a regime on the road to normalization. . . .

In the weakening and collapse of totalitarian regimes, external factors do not bear the same importance across the board. They were decisive in the case of Nazi Germany, which was crushed by multiple armies. On the other hand, the "capitalist" world rarely constituted a danger for communist regimes. Nazism increased the legitimacy of communism in the eyes of the West. During the era known as the Cold War, the "rollback" policy was immediately dismissed in favor of containment. This option did not prevent vast communist expansions in Asia, Africa, and even in the Americas. In the end, the only place on earth where communism was overthrown the way Nazism had been—by a massive, bona fide invasion (albeit amidst a chorus of protests from a number of noncommunist powers)—was on the minuscule island of Grenada.

CHAPTER 4
THEOLOGY

THERE COMES A point in a study of this nature when one has to step away from historical analysis if one wants to do justice to the experience of human beings. In fact, when faced with the excess of iniquity, human hearts were overwhelmed and the limits of reason were exceeded; humanity was confronted with a new and unknown beast without historical precedent. The great witnesses of the twentieth century have for the most part cried out to heaven. Some judged that it was empty, others that one could implore it, plead with it, and hope. In actual fact, when one reads Orwell, Andrei Platonov, Anna Akhmatova, Osip Mandelstam, and Levi, one senses that these two responses to the metaphysical challenge cohabit or obscurely alternate within the same souls.

EVIL

Plotinus defined evil as "the privation of good." The scholastics modified this to "the privation of a good that is due." Blindness, for example, is an evil, because it belongs to man to have sight. If he is incapable of seeing the invisible, even though he has good eyes, he cannot complain because sight is not made to see things beyond a limited field. The idea, therefore, is that evil is negatively defined. It is pure nothingness—a hole in being. But it seems to me that this definition does not adequately account for the horror that gripped human beings in the face of what communism and Nazism inflicted on them.

What caused this horror was less evil than, more profoundly, the will to evil. Man naturally wants to be happy. His will is generally turned towards what he considers to be his good. Since his imagination is small, it is readily understandable—as most ancient philosophers have explained—that man is easily mistaken about his good. This leads him to commit bad actions because he does not see what this might cost him. Stealing obviously brings a good, fornicating produces a pleasure, killing appeases anger, and lying might enable one to escape from a tight situation. The price must nonetheless be paid. However, there is another category of acts, acts that seem inhumanly disinterested, that are not followed by any pleasure imaginable to the ordinary man. Those who commit such acts seem attracted by the sheer transgression of the rule. They are frightening because we do not understand them and because they appear to have abandoned our common humanity. We understand very well the thief, the fornicator, and the murderer: we find points of correspondence in our souls, we do not have to dig too deeply into ourselves to find some greed, lust, and violence. But faced with this other category of acts, we are as disconcerted as we would be before a miracle; indeed, it represents an inverse miracle, a negative exception to the known laws of nature. Man wants his good, but in this case there is no conceivable good. That is why those who suffered under communism and Nazism, even those who merely studied them with some application, have been perpetually haunted by the question: why? Why compromise the war effort, spend money, congest transportation, and mobilize men to go hunt down and put to death a little Jewish girl hiding in an attic? Why—when there is no longer any organized opposition, when everyone is submissive and obedient—arrest millions of people? Why mobilize the police and judicial systems to make people confess to crimes that are unimaginable and obviously absurd? And once they have confessed, why gather other people to make them put on a show of indignation and participate in the execution? Why shoot half the general officer corps on the eve of a well-planned war?

But what seemed most incomprehensible of all is that these enormous and inept crimes were committed by ordinary—even particularly ordinary—people. These people were of ordinary intelligence and morality. Occasionally, the vast crowd of executioners contained individuals who were perverse by character, sadists who took pleasure in making others suffer. But these were the exception. Of course, actual perverts prospered and were used for certain tasks—but this only up to a certain point, beyond which they were removed, and sometimes punished, in the name of good discipline. In their desire to understand, victims could no longer cling to explanations based on the wickedness of which man is capable and is often the bearer. One had to look further for the answer, to the "system" itself. But however crazy, the rationality of the system was refuted by these self-destructive actions that went against the interest of the project.

This is why the criminal personalities of some leaders—of Stalin above all—were considered favorably and earned them a certain gratitude: they lent a certain element of humanity, offered an explanation, and restored coherence. Because history offers numerous examples of criminal tyrants, precedents existed. There was nothing new under the sun; anxiety in face of the unknown was thereby alleviated. But as the most lucid people knew, the so-called tyrant was not a tyrant because he did not act with his personal good in mind. He was himself tyrannized by something of a higher order. It therefore seemed to follow that the crime must be linked to insanity. But this was no ordinary insanity such as had been seen in insane tyrants, because insanity includes an accidental element that provides for spaces where rest and play are possible. (This is why Romanians were amused for a short while by the antics of the Ceausescus.) Ideological insanity, at its worst moments, created a solid block that lacked the slightest crevice in which to take refuge. Here, everything went wrong.

THE DEMON AND THE PERSON

Thus, even minds that were hardly religious were spontaneously tempted to look beyond the intelligible human order and glimpse the higher governance of a different order. Not only the weight of injustice and proximity of evil, but their inability to compare them to anything known impelled them to put questions to heaven. They were brought to this point because both regimes professed an active hatred of all religions that honored a divine order distinct from the one established by men. Nazism hated the God of Abraham; communism hated every type of god and especially God. In both cases, the religious organization of conquered countries was immediately overturned. It was sometimes annihilated (Albania proclaimed itself the first atheist country on earth); more often, it was subjugated and perverted. Christians, Jews, Muslims, Buddhists, Taoists, and Confucians were persecuted, and their persecution was not temporary but permanent. Although it had no political utility—indeed, it had numerous disadvantages—it lasted until the very end.

This is why several martyrs of these regimes saw the action of an extrahuman, "angelic" order at work, and believed it to be capable of exercising a direct power. This power was not really mediated by an evil human will, but rather acted through humans without their knowing it—or in such a way that they knew only confusedly what they were doing. Anesthetizing common sense and moral conscience, this power transformed a man, subjected to a sort of magic spell, into a puppet whose strings it controlled. According to this intuition, the ultimate tyrant is neither Hitler, nor Lenin, nor Mao, but the Prince of This World in person.

In person: the term is ambiguous. Boethius defined the person in a way that has gained wide currency, as "an individual substance of a rational nature." In this theological tradition, this created substance, if it loses its orientation toward both its Creator and its own end, undergoes contradictions that mutilate and destroy it. Because nothing concrete is known about the angelic world, one can speculate that by virtue of his higher rank, the evil angel is devoured more thoroughly by his evil will than man. The act of annihilation he produces is first carried out on himself in such a way that his substance—a term which for us human beings evokes a nature that is positive, indestructible, and spoiled (but not destroyed) by sin—is gradually reduced to his pure will to evil. Because of his greater capacity for evil, what remains of the natural *suppositum* in him—the person—asymptotically approaches impersonality. The fallen angelic person could sustain the maximum degree of impersonality.

This is undoubtedly speculation, but it lends credence to the notion of an impersonal person that one finds so universally in the literature of witnesses who were stifled by the dullness, meagerness, and banality of those who caused them to suffer and die. Equally impersonal is the whole hierarchy of power, up to and including its summit. Witnesses were also amazed at the contrast between the incredible destructive power of these apparatuses—so wonderfully clever, and capable of going into the greatest detail—and their incredible incapacity to organize, construct, or simply allow the existence of the barest necessities of life, even of what was necessary for these apparatuses to survive.

Who holds power in a pure Nazi or communist regime? We would have thought that this question would be easier to answer for these regimes than for any others, simply because the holder of all power was visible, even hauntingly visible, everywhere—the führer, the secretary general, the party. Yet this query represented a profound enigma to those capable of philosophic reflection: to

Junger, Platonov, Orwell, Milosz, Zinoviev. . . . They suggested what such religious souls as Mandelstam, Akhmatova, Bulgakov, Rauschning, Herbert, and Solzhenitsyn also proclaimed: it was the devil! He was the one who communicated his inhuman impersonality to his subjects. Dostoyevsky and Vladimir Soloviev had intuited it in advance. Thus, to fail to mention this personage would be to fail to listen faithfully to all these testimonies, and yet we must still observe caution with regard to the mysterious force they have named and of which they knew the proximity through first-hand experience.

SALVATION

The biblical imprint on communism and Nazism is nowhere more evident than in the will they share to *save* the world, even when the means to such salvation included the obliteration of all biblical influences. In "pagan" religions, the natural order contains the divine idea within itself and is sufficient to cause it to be conceived. Here, the natural order is equivalent to the divine order. One has only to contemplate, to recognize, to imitate it. Ancient philosophy— and as far as I know, Indian and Chinese as well—did not promise universal salvation, but only that of a small elite group, which, by means of long and difficult spiritual exercises, would attain the capacity to live happily and in conformity with the eternal order of nature. The idea of salvation, insofar as it presupposes an "exodus" from the world or the idea of "changing" the world as a whole, is inconceivable for such a philosophy.

Marxist-Leninist salvation is optimistic. It is comparable to the salvation proclaimed in biblical prophecy. Its goal is to overcome nature and humanity such as they are, to arrive at a messianic era of peace and justice in which the wolf and the lamb graze together and the discipline and frustrations of marriage, family, property, law, and penury are abolished. Death itself is vanquished: reveries on this theme in the early days of the Bolshevik revolution were nourished by the speculations of a certain Fedorov, an enthusiast of the scientific resurrection of the body and immortality. The "new man" to be produced by socialism is a sort of glorified body, such as had been glimpsed in prophecy. But now, salvation is entrusted to human hands and is to be obtained through political means: *non Domino sed nobis.*

Today, only a small minority believes in the existence of divine commandments. For this group of believers (which once included many Jews and Christians who later became communist), the contradiction between *progress,* which man controls, and biblical teaching should be immediately obvious. Believers cannot accept the concept of progress, understood as a deep transformation of human existence through the action of history or of a politico-historical will; they cannot accept it because it attributes to political action a transformation that depends, according to the Bible, on divine grace alone. When what is possible only for divine action becomes the goal of human action, this action attempts the impossible. Violent action against nature fails and soon transforms itself into the destruction of nature and, with it, humanity. Pelagius thought that man could save himself to a certain degree by force of will and ascetic discipline. Saint Augustine retorted that the Pelagians simply oppressed themselves without thereby improving themselves. The same might be said of the "positive hero" of Bolshevik legend. In fact, the latter is worse: whereas the Pelagian intended to attain virtue according to the common meaning of the term, the "positive hero" sought virtue as defined by ideology— which is to say, he sought vice. Moreover, ancient Pelagianism, like ancient philosophy, aimed only at the progress of the individual. The new kind is collectivized. The transfer of the Pelagian idea to political power is more destructive: now it is the other (or all the others) who is to be corrected by education or, if necessary, by re-education in a yard surrounded by barbed wire.

In contrast to communist salvation, Nazi salvation is pessimistic. It requires humanity to overcome the illusions it had ingested with the poison of the Bible, especially of the Gospel, that fruit of "resentment." The point is to return to a natural order conceived in the black light of a romantic-tragic sensibility, to rediscover the original purity of earth and blood, corrupted by commercial and technical society and by the bastardizing mixture of races. The appeal of Nazism is addressed to heroes who are prepared to die, to those who have renounced the illusion of truth and justice and are ready to follow the will of the race, of the *Volk*, incarnated in the leader, to the very end. The superman is an impassive knight, loyal whether conqueror or conquered, but always noble and beautiful. As we now know, this ideal in fact led to a regiment of brainless SS, a hierarchy of scoundrels with a madman at the peak, and a stupid war of annihilation.

These two opposed doctrines nevertheless have in common the idea of a collective salvation coming in history, a biblical idea that is contrary to the historical understanding of ancient, Indian, and Chinese philosophies. Upon this framework, the two doctrines pile a hodgepodge of notions lifted from the natural and historical sciences, thereby transforming the immense knowledge accumulated in the nineteenth century into a *supernaturally* impoverished mental automatism. It is not in fact consistent with the nature of human intelligence that these two insane systems should have presented themselves as its product. It does not make sense that so many normal and sometimes superior minds—professors, scholars, thinkers capable of eminence—should have been subject to such paralysis and deformation of common sense. Psychiatric explanations are no less metaphorical than the image used with reference to Nazism: that of the Pied Piper of Hamelin. But if one evokes this legend, one is very close to naming the one standing behind the Piper. According to Scripture, it is the "father of lies," the "murderer and liar from the beginning."

NAZI "BIBLICISM"

It has been said that Gobineau and Nietzsche, to whom the Nazis sometimes appealed, were not anti-Semites. It is true that they claimed to admire the Jews. Gobineau considered them a "superior race," an "aristocracy." Nietzsche admired them because they had not dissolved into the mass of "last men" generated by democracy. For Nietzsche, moreover, anti-Semitism was associated with democratic vulgarity. But one does not have to dig very deep beneath this superficial admiration to find envy and jealousy. In German nationalism, exaltation of the nation imitated the form of the providential election of the Jewish people. Owing nothing to Providence, the German election was deemed the product of history and of nature. According to this idea, the German people are heirs of the great tradition of all humanity passed down from people to people. (Russian nationalism contented itself with transposing what had been promised to Germanic peoples to the Slavs and the Russians.)

Since nature and soil are the bases of election, it makes sense that the Jewish people should be the living negation of nature and soil. This was emphasized by the young Hegel: "the first act by which Abraham became the father of a nation [was] a rupture that breaks the bonds of common life and of love, all binding relationships within which he had lived with men and nature up to that point." "Abraham was a stranger on the earth. . . . The whole world, to which he stood in absolute opposition, was sustained in existence by a God who remained foreign to it, a God in whom no element of nature could participate. . . . It is only by the grace of God that he entered into a relationship with the world. . . . It was impossible for him to love anything." "There was in the jealous God of Abraham and of his descendants the astounding requirement that he and his nation be the only ones to have a God."

The relationship of the Jews to God cuts them off from humanity. They can belong to no community, because the sacred character of any community (such as in the Eleusinian mysteries) remains forever foreign to them: "they neither see nor hear it." Nor do they participate in epic heroism. "In Egypt, great things are accomplished for the Jews, but *they themselves* undertake no heroic actions; for them, Egypt undergoes all kinds of calamities and miseries, and it is in the midst of a universal lament that they withdraw before the pursuit of the unfortunate Egyptians. But they experience only the cunning joy of the coward whose enemy is found fallen without any help from him." Thus, their last act in Egypt is a "theft."[1]

Hegel considers the Jews' claim to election intolerable, as he does the absolute dependence they confess with respect to a God he judges (at least in his youth—later, his view evolved) to be a stranger to man, an enemy of man's nobility and his liberty. Because it contained the idea of this God, the spirit of Abraham makes the Jew the "unique favorite," a conviction that is also the root of the Jew's "contempt for the whole world." As declared slaves of their God, the Jews cannot accede to the dignity of the free man: "The Greeks were supposed to be equal because all were free; the Jews, because *all* were incapable of independence." This is why Hegel, openly Marcionite, considers the Christian God to differ fundamentally from the Jewish: "Jesus fought against not only a part of Jewish destiny; for he was aligned with no other element, but opposed it in its entirety."

Hegel translates into the grand tones of philosophy the conscious or unconscious feelings of the pagan soul in the presence of the supernatural mystery of Israel—a mystery it indeed experiences as alien, as inimical to all nature. The same feelings also exist in the souls of the baptized. These obscure effects were conceptualized in German thought better than elsewhere. Harnack, the great theological authority of Wilhelmine Germany and liberal European Protestantism, gave a series of lectures at the University of Berlin that was later published under the title *The Essence of Christianity*. This essence unfolds in four great historical moments: the Jewish, the Greek, the Latin, and finally, the German, its purest fulfillment.[2]

Harnack authored a book favorable to Marcion, and he did not hesitate to compare it with the work of Martin Luther, the founder of "German Christianity." The Russians, for their part, produced an abundant literature on Russian Christianity, on the Russian Christ, even on Christ-Russia. Léon Bloy and Charles Péguy made the case for God's special preference for France. But in this last country, the anti-Jewish theme was not orchestrated by great minds, but only by the mediocre.

From the heights of German philosophy, the anti-Jewish theme then descended into the low and foolish souls of Nazi leaders. Consider these words of Hitler, caricaturing Hegel before Rauschning:

> The Jew is a creature of another God. It must be that he stems from another human stock. The Aryan and the Jew: I oppose one to the other, and if I give one the name of man, I am obliged to give a different name to the other. They are as far removed from one another as an animal species from humans. It's not that I call the Jew an animal: he is much further removed from the animal than are we Aryans. He is a being alien to the natural order, a being outside nature.[3]

Rauschning further reports the following statement: "There cannot be two elect peoples. We are the people of God." This is pure rhetoric, since Hitler was perfectly atheist as to a Jewish or Christian God. But it shows how Hitler's outrageous anti-Semitism takes the biblical form of a *perversa imatitio* of the sacred history of the Jews. The Aryan people, the Elect, the chosen Germanic race purifies the German soil just as Israel purified the soil of Canaan. This is the first stage in the history of salvation. The second is the elimination of a Judaized Christianity, which represents the fulfillment of Jewish cowardice and democratic bastardization. The third is the triumph of those magnanimous souls who might still be said to belong to

Germanized Christianity, or, better still, to the religion of the pre-Christian natural pantheon. As mangled by the Nazi ideology, Nietzsche and Wagner (in mutilated and brutalized form) might be proposed as the patrons of this new culture.

COMMUNIST "BIBLICISM"

While Nazism offers a counterfeit of the Old Testament, communism offers a counterfeit of both Old and New Testaments. The *perversa imitatio* of Judaism and Christianity, which constitutes its "charm," is well enough known that a few words will suffice to characterize it.

This ideology proposes a mediator and a redeemer. The "proletariat," the "exploited," those who have nothing, will open the door of liberation to the world. The proletariat is to the other classes what Israel is among the nations, what the "remnant of Israel" is to Israel itself. It is the suffering servant of Isaiah and it is the Christ. It is the fruit of naturalized history, just as the other was the fruit of sacred history. In all these ways, communism is seductive for Jews as well as for Christians who believe they recognize in it the Good News proclaimed to the poor and the lowly. It is a form of universalism, since there is no longer Jew or Greek, slave or free man, man or woman—just as Saint Paul promised. It abolishes national barriers, which is equivalent to the salvation promised to the "nations." It brings the peace and justice of the messianic kingdom, overcomes the regime of interests, and dries up the "frozen waters of egoistic calculation." A Kantian disinterestedness, that pure love described by Fénelon, will flourish in this new climate.

Communism promised Jews that it would eliminate the burden of the commandments, the hedge of the Torah, as well as end their separation from the nations. By removing the weight of being Jewish, it would also remove the permanent causes of oppression. It was an alternative to Jewish life that did not involve a passage to Christianity or to the equally disdained Islam (which, as history had shown, did not in fact protect them, since the mark of Judaism remained after conversion). Communism was thus an entry into a new world that did not require formal treason or apostasy, since the religious goal of the Torah—peace and justice—was supposed to be guaranteed. The Jewish community, moreover, could continue to exist ideally. The name "Jew" could be carried without shame. No longer involving a particular responsibility or special obligation, it would simply mark a glorious origin, since, as an oppressed people, the Jews were related to the "proletariat." Finally, the passage to communism—the Exodus, one is tempted to say—appeared as the culmination of a process of emancipation and secularization that had proved irresistible throughout the preceding century.

Christians, for their part, were summoned to disavow their faith in God directly. Yet that faith had already been ready to fall like a ripe fruit. Attacked in successive waves since the beginning of the Enlightenment, the Christian faith had found it more and more difficult to defend its rational status. After Leibniz, no great mind felt constrained by the authority of dogma or searched for truth in exploring it more deeply. If certain great authors like Kant and Hegel still confessed the Christian faith, they nonetheless gave it a rational interpretation within the framework of their systems; or, like Rousseau, Kierkegaard, or Dostoyevsky, they proclaimed its utter irrationality. Alternatively, they hoped to deduce it from the requirements of morality, practical action, and cultural production. But Christianity was flushed out of this last refuge by the communist idea, with its good arguments that accused Christianity of being the opium of the people. Christianity was deemed an illusory escape, an impotent consolation in the face of a condition of injustice to which it, by its mere existence, was an accomplice. For a whole century—from Lamennais to Tolstoy and beyond—an important part of Christian thought was tempted to fuse with humanitarianism. Presenting itself as more truly Christian, the latter was animated with an enthusiasm and fervor that had deserted traditional religion. To become a communist brought the feeling of having finally fulfilled, in a realistic fashion, the commandment to love one's neighbor. At the same time, reason was reassured by having been established anew on the sure foundation of science.

HERESIES

The Christian religion has been unstable since its birth. It contains a tangle of difficulties and plentiful motives for doubt; constant effort is required to maintain its equilibrium. But the crises that have successively arisen, although prompted by historical circumstances, generally follow a regular pattern. Along the mountain of Christianity, one finds certain paths that avalanches have followed since the earliest centuries of our era—and they are still vulnerable in our day. The great inaugural heresies are embraced anew by movements that believe themselves to be new and by men who are unaware they are following ancient tendencies. They do not know that they walk in the footsteps of heretics whose names they ignore, and they are even more oblivious of the doctrinal bond that ties them to such ancients.

In the present case, the heretical paths happen to be the oldest of Christianity: gnosticism, Marcionism, and millenarianism.

To be sure, gnosticism is not specifically Christian. Also parasitical upon Judaism and Islam, it covers such a vast territory that I can only allude to it here. As I have said, Marxist-Leninism is above all an overarching vision of the naturo-historical world as one polarized between good and evil as discerned by those initiated in the true knowledge. These men penetrate other men's minds with saving knowledge and move the world in the direction of their definitive good. This fundamental structure can be seen in most forms of gnosticism—in particular those that so horrified Saint John in the days of Cerinthus or Saint Irenaeus in the days of Valentinus. Starting with Marx, this gnostic kernel was claimed to be based on positive science. But the fact that it lost its mythological luxuriance, its poetic coloration, and declined into the prosaic harping of Lenin does not mean that the gnostic core was eliminated. It is true that many "progressive Christians" wanted to revive a primitive religious allure and could not understand why communism militantly insisted on its atheism. These same Christians approved of its practical program and its "method of analysis," as they said—that is, of its theory as a whole. Others finally accepted this atheism by a kind of reverse "leap of faith," as their supreme sacrifice to the persuasive logic of communism.

Marcionism, a species of the genus gnosticism, belongs to the world of Christianity. It was a precocious historical product (early second century) of the contentious separation between the church and the synagogue. Marcion believed that the God of Abraham, the Creator and Judge, was not the same as the God of Love, the Savior whose emanation was Jesus. Thus, he amputated the Old Testament from the canon of Scripture, as well as that part of the New Testament that was directly bound up with it. In this way Christian revelation was dissociated from Mosaic revelation. Marcion thus denied that the latter recorded the historical stages leading to the coming of the Messiah. The Marcionite Messiah does not find his proofs or genealogy in biblical prophecy: his legitimacy depends entirely on the persuasive value of a "message" extracted from the Gospel (an expurgated Gospel, moreover) and from gnostic mythological additions completing the Gospel and guiding its interpretation. Marcion's Christ brings an anticosmic and antinomian message of an alien, sublime, heroic, and paradoxical morality. Its mission is to replace the common morality that the biblical commandments had ratified. Thus, according to Marcion, hell includes the righteous of the Old Testament, who were servants of the Creator God, whereas the Savior God receives into his paradise the Sodomites and Egyptians, who had refused to bow before the ancient law. In this heresy, the Jews appear as representatives of the bygone world and an obsolete morality—the work of the bad god.

Gnosticism and Marcionism, always allied, have never ceased to exercise the Christian imagination and to subvert Christian thought.

Condemned at their birth as the worst of heresies, they have nevertheless remained a permanent temptation that arises repeatedly from century to century, and never so much as in our own time. They mark the weak point of the teaching, that crack in the ground of faith that has allowed so many Christians to fall for the political gnosticism of communism and the frantic Marcionism of Nazism.

Since the two heresies were always intimately linked, their association brought about a new point of contact between Nazism and communism.

In gnostic communism, the historical scheme openly replaces the biblical meaning of history in that both the Creator God and the Savior God are rejected: the first is replaced by the natural history of humanity, and the second by the willed action of the party. The assault against the Christian church was therefore immediate, and produced more martyrs in a few years than it had in the entire time since its birth. But all gods and all religions were equally enemies, which meant that the synagogue was also attacked, as well as the very idea of community. From the end of the '30s onward, anti-Semitism pure and simple succeeded the earlier anti-Judaism. After 1945, it was forbidden to single out Jews among the "victims of fascism," or even to mention the Shoah. And from the moment Zionism announced itself as an independent national movement, it was also forbidden to tolerate Zionism. Communism is jealous and does not accept "other gods before it."

Nazism focused on the Marcionite version of gnosticism. It formally and provisionally accepted a "German" Christianity, which invoked a God other than that of Abraham. It persecuted faithful Christians and tried to enrich itself by drawing upon fin-de-siècle esotericism and occultism. It sought to awaken the neopaganism of the old German gods, thereby wronging what had been honorable and beautiful in Germanic mythology—what it had in common with Homer—through its counterfeits.

The third heresy that came into play was millenarianism. Aiming at a radical change within history, millenarianism was an outgrowth and accompaniment of messianism. Biblical messianism awaited the coming of a royal figure capable of restoring a covenant of peace in Israel and among the nations. Primitive Christian millenarianism believed that Christ would return to earth to reign gloriously with the resurrected righteous ones for a thousand years. In the twentieth century, these doctrines underwent certain secularizing alterations. The messianic idea contaminated the most extreme forms of nationalism: the German or Russian people was seen to carry the final redemptive hopes of human history. And modern history has been shaken by the heroic crises of millenarianism. Consisting in an impatience to bring about the Kingdom of God and a will to take charge of its advent, millenarianism can be understood as a sort of heightened, collectivized, and politicized Pelagianism. The Taborites of Bohemia, the Anabaptists of Münster, the extremist wing of the English Revolution, Sabbatai Zevi—such crises become all the bloodier when, disburdened of the idea of God, they envision the instauration of a *regnum hominis*.

In the two systems of salvation, communist and Nazi, it is hard to sort out whether the Christians detested the Jews for being their root or the Jews hated the Christians for being their offspring. Whatever the order, first one then the other fell victim to persecution. But this too is noteworthy: relations between Jews and Christians are almost always poisoned by the very persons who have apostatized from their respective religions and left no trace of them beyond a mutual hatred.

CHAPTER 5
MEMORY

I WISH NOW to consider parallels between the work of memory concerning Nazism on the one hand and communism on the other, considering the question mainly from the standpoint of religion. To this point, I have done this only from the standpoint of politics. But the gravity of the events brought on by these two movements, as I have said, engages religious consciousness. The spectrum of positions is as broad in the case of religion as it was for politics, but it is also different. The two do not coincide.

I will consider paganism, by which I understand what is not derived, or is no longer derived, from the biblical sources of Judaism and Christianity. We can note at the outset that there is room for different, even opposing attitudes within each of these categories.

"PAGAN" OBLIVION OF COMMUNISM

Let us take the example of China. The horizon of its philosophical and religious traditions (which are closely mingled) is an impersonal cosmos. Normally and ideally governed by harmony, this cosmos is still vulnerable to disorder, even to a momentary return to chaos. More than European history, Chinese history is punctuated by extraordinarily violent cataclysms that are capable of reducing the population by half. As late as the nineteenth century, the Taiping Rebellion was able directly or indirectly to cause the death of seventy million Chinese—a catastrophe equivalent to that of the Mao years. In both cases, a charismatic leader and a party were rendered fanatical by a syncretistic doctrine that included elements alien to the tradition (Christian elements in the Taiping Rebellion, Marxist ones later on). Their fanaticism ultimately caused the Chinese order to collapse into a bottomless chaos.

These historical and political catastrophes could be compared to the natural catastrophes—floods, earthquakes, poor harvests—that capriciously shake the Chinese earth. One gets the impression— perhaps the superficial impression of a distant observer—that all it takes is that the situation improve, that bellies be full again, that pleasures return, in order for it again to be possible to be enterprising and to make money, in order for the fabric of society to begin a quasi-biological process of scarring and for life's rediscovered dynamism to render the work of memory superfluous. Moreover, the Chinese regime, which remains formally communist, still controls information about the past. One might say from afar that the permanence of the cosmos—at once close to home and stretching far beyond these perturbations—softens the sense of history. A historical account thereby gains the feel of a meteorological report; it is part of a regular cycle troubled by storms.

CHRISTIAN OBLIVION OF COMMUNISM

In theory, the Christian world should have felt concerned and even responsible in face of the communist project. The idea of a history aimed at universal salvation developed in a Christian environment, after all; here, the expectation of a definitive liberation, general purification, and triumph of the good was honed. And yet, the perversion of these same ideas had never brought about such iniquity; never had sin filled the earth to such a degree. Here was something to reflect on. But the Christian world not only forgot communism, but, on the urging of its pastors, considered its forgetting an act of piety.

In fact, Christians in general—and post-Christians even more—reacted like "pagans" to the extent that they distinguished themselves only weakly from nonbelievers. Their baptism proved to be more or less superficial, as has always been the case. Communism endured for so long that it came to resemble a kind of ice age, a series of exceptionally cold winters. The climate having warmed up again, we give it no thought and benefit from the sunlight to take up our daily tasks.

But there is also a properly Christian oblivion that must be considered—or rather, two opposite ways of forgetting. The first is rooted in the primordial soil of the Christian faith, particularly in the sense of evil and sin. On the one hand, Christians have been taught they are sinners; that sin—original and personal—has accompanied the good in human life from the beginning and today more than ever. They have also been taught that they proceed from Christ's cross, in other words, from a history in which all men collectively committed the greatest conceivable evil in putting to death the only one who was absolutely innocent. The Word, God Himself, was vanquished between a Friday and a Sunday. But by this same history, they are also forgiven, reconciled, albeit forever subject to sin. The Christian's familiarity with sin and the good means that he is less surprised by one or the other: he always expects sin and forgiveness, and there is no sin so serious that it cannot be forgiven with the help of repentance. In this case, then, forgetting is the expected consequence of forgiveness.

Beside this virtuous oblivion—or perhaps in its place—there may be another forgetfulness that is not virtuous. Normally, forgiveness has value only if it has been asked of God and the victim, if the sin has already been recognized and the request articulated. If these conditions are not met and forgiveness is still granted unilaterally, there is a good chance that it is invalid. But this would constitute an additional sin. This all-too-easy forgiveness might arise from a sublime morality that dispenses with justice and invites the self-congratulation of great souls. It might be a matter of simple laziness in the examination of facts, or a lack of courage in face of the requirements of justice. Or it might arise from a repugnance for examining one's own complicity—whether active or passive—with those one forgives. This occurs all the more easily in that one also affords oneself absolution. Whatever the case may be, no one seems to be preparing a public ceremony of repentance on the subject of communism.

The extraordinary amnesty from which communist crimes have benefited seems to me to arise from this second sort of oblivion. Even though more martyrs to the faith emerged under communism than in any other epoch of the church's history, no one seems eager to establish this.

Communism was fed by a massive Christian apostasy. It is not clear that this apostasy—not to mention the compromises of principle and more and less serious acts of complicity—is considered to be really blameworthy. Communists are generally held to have committed venial missteps and are often praised for their generous intentions. The reason for it is simple: Christians have not yet been completely purged of communist ideas, which have mixed with humanitarian ideas in their minds and been introduced among the faithful and the clergy. In dissimulated and unconscious form, such ideas are still active along the lines of the "heretical" tendencies cited above. Even today, one still hears talk of a "third way" between capitalism and socialism. We have not yet understood that to subsume our world under the concept of "capitalism" is already to enter into the dichotomous worldview of ideology—even if we think we are far from it. The fact is that part of the Christian world still does not clearly know what it is we should remember.

JEWISH OBLIVION OF COMMUNISM

What we have just said concerning Christian oblivion also applies to Jews—except, of course, things relating to the core of faith. Communism is not a Jewish invention. It is easier to trace its origins back to Christianity than to Judaism, which in this case only fell in line with Christianity. But many Jews rallied to the cause from its birth in the middle of the nineteenth century. They then continued to associate with it with the same zeal and unshakable conviction, thus abandoning their community, history, and faith—just as Christians abandoned theirs.

These Jews played a significant role in this project, but it was seldom a principal one. In 1917, the majority of Russia's Jews did not follow the Bolshevik Party. They were its victims as much as others were. Those who did belong to the party occupied high positions, but were subordinated more and more as anti-Semitism developed. That said, the crimes of personages such as Iagoda, Kaganovitch, and many others in Russia and Central and Eastern Europe rival the most frightening of the century. This case also calls for remembrance and repentance—at least if one considers apostate Jews to be Jews. But so far, amnesty and oblivion appear to be just as widespread and consciences just as peaceful as in Christendom.

JEWISH MEMORY OF NAZISM

As we take up this subject, it seems appropriate to underscore a point that has rarely been noticed. From the time the Jews re-entered the history of the West through their emancipation at the end of the eighteenth century, Jewish people—or at least some of its members—have joined in all the undertakings, both good and bad, of the peoples with whom they were mixed. Throughout this history (both happy and disastrous), in its intellectual, political, social, and economic aspects, the Jews have been present. But they were not, by definition, present in the history of Nazism. With the possible exception of communism, this enterprise was one more purely devoted to evil than any other in this century. But the Jews were victims, not guilty parties. The biblical prophets would have considered this a great blessing, since their lesson was that death is preferable to such a sin. The Jews, therefore, were exempt from a temptation to which others among the "nations" succumbed in great numbers. From this point of view they are justified in their sense of being innocent and set apart from others.

Where Nazism is concerned, two extrinsic factors exacerbate Jewish memory. Since Nazism presented itself as the declared enemy of democracy—whereas communism claims to be its fulfillment—it is the negative pole by which the democratic movement defined itself after 1945, when it accelerated and became universal. Moreover, having been classified as the extreme right, Nazism has been the foil par excellence of the left. In occupied France, there was compromise and complicity and a fascist regime established during the war. Here in particular, then, the left sought to claim a monopoly on "anti-fascism"—which is confused, according to the communist vulgate, with anti-Nazism. The French left has an interest in aligning Jewish opinion with itself by outbidding all parties where this memory is concerned. But this has the effect of carrying the topic onto terrains that have more to do with leftism than with the interests of the Jewish community.

Jewish memory is justifiably alarmed by currents of thought that directly offend it. Holocaust denial is the extreme type of such an offense. It departs so far from truth and from historical good sense that only a few individuals without the least intellectual authority subscribe to it. It is unfortunate that this notion is prohibited in France by a law—and by one that was sponsored by the Communist Party. A question of truth should not be legally removed from the normal field of discussion. Those who deny the most solidly attested facts are thereby enabled to complain, even to claim a violation of their freedom of thought, and thus to escape the dishonor to which this freedom would expose them.

The banalization of the Shoah is another cause of grief. In everyday usage, the word "genocide" has been abused by an unwarranted extension. It is applied to every act of bullying, serious or not—and before long, no doubt, to the carnage of baby seals or to whale-hunting.

Men have massacred each other from the time they were numerous enough to fight. Ancient laws of war provided for the death of men of fighting age and the enslavement of women and children. If we adopt the current usage, the Trojan War and the Punic Wars were genocides. Euripides, in *The Trojan Women,* and Thucydides describe genocides in their reports of the punishment of the Meleans. The *Drang nach Osten* of the German High Middle Ages eliminated several Slavic and Baltic peoples between the Elbe and the Oder. Now that modern weapons have replaced assegai, tribal African wars have caused millions of deaths in a few months. Who today remembers the Scythians, the Sarmatians, the Avars, the Pechenegs, or the Khazars—all of them peoples that knew days of glory, but are now wiped out down to the last soul?

A massacre is not genocide. In the legal usage ratified by international convention, genocide is defined as "the methodical destruction of an ethnic group." But this is a clumsy definition: many massacres, such as those I have just cited, would fall under this definition. Moreover, if one questions classifying the Jews as an "ethnic group"—which was the Nazi position—then the Shoah does not count as genocide!

To remain in the realm of historical fact and within the limits of the twentieth century, let us posit that genocide, as distinct from a simple massacre, requires the following criterion: the killing must have been premeditated in the framework of an ideology. That ideology, in turn, must have as a goal the annihilation of part of humanity in order to bring about its conception of the good. The planned destruction must encompass the entirety of the targeted group—even if the plan is not brought to a conclusion for reasons of material impossibility or political reversal. The only known precedent might well be the Vendeans, which, according to the orders (December 1793) of the revolutionary National Convention, were supposed to be "destroyed" entirely. Carrier wrote: "It is by the principle of humanity that I purge the earth of the freedom of these monsters." As it turned out, a good quarter of the population was purged in the zone of destruction—a number that approaches those of the twentieth-century performances.

In applying this criterion, we can begin by distinguishing the Nazi genocide of the Jews and the gypsies—to which we could add that of the handicapped whom Hitler disposed of on the eve of the war. I would also add the Ukrainian genocide of 1932–33, which resembles the genocide of the Vendeans to the extent that it was carried out at a time when the peasants had given up all resistance and was interrupted when the political goal was deemed to have been attained. Let us also add the genocide of the Armenians in 1915 and the Cambodian one. All these genocides were planned in advance and shrouded in secrecy. Although the secrecy did not resist military defeat or the fall of the regimes responsible, it has persisted to some degree. The secret of the Ukrainian genocide, for example, has been penetrated only confidentially and is even today far from having been documented with precision. It is generally thought to have caused between five and seven million deaths. And there are grounds for thinking that there have been other genocides still—ones of which we have not yet heard.

The Armenian genocide, while undeniable, remains somewhat in the category of the "classic" massacre. The Young Turks hoped to make their country a nation on the Jacobin model. In order to achieve unity, they mobilized Ottoman mercenaries, thereby following an old recipe for power they had already applied several times, particularly against these very Armenians in 1895. This recipe inherited the pitiless rules of ancient warfare. The Japanese did the same thing in China. The Ukrainian and Jewish genocides, for their part, are based solely on ideological projects, and thus fall under the same genus. In the first case, the point was to extend and perfect communist control by annihilating resistance based on national feeling—or simply the Ukrainian nation itself. Once this goal had been achieved, "liquidation" of the rest of the population was no longer necessary or even desirable in view of the larger project. On the eve of his death, Stalin was considering resuming the operation. In the case of the Nazis, the project of racial purity implied putting to death all Jews, without exception. On this point, the Nazi genocides resembled such traditional ones as the Armenian genocide-massacre in particular—ones in which women and children formed pyramids of corpses. More recently, there has also been the massacre of the Tutsis by the Hutus in Rwanda.

And yet there is a difference. In fact, the immense majority of Jews—but not only of Jews—are aware of an irreducible difference between what happened to them and what happened to other peoples. There is an ineradicable but obscure awareness, a source of permanent questioning that yields no unified answer.

A number of Jewish voices, including some of the most distinguished—beginning with Raymond Aron, Boris Souvarine, and Hannah Arendt—have considered the two horrors of the century with an equable eye and impartial judgment. The recent noble article by Anne Applebaum, "A Dearth of Feeling," refutes in advance the opinion of those who imply that the Jews, egoistically turned in on their pain, remain insensitive to the pain of others.[1] In one of her very last texts, Annie Kriegel made a point of recalling that, in the case of Stalinism, certain Jews were better off not to have cultivated the legend of their "fundamental innocence as victims" too far.[2]

Yet, among those I have just cited, I do not believe that awareness of difference is completely extinguished by the spirit of justice. For this awareness to be completely obliterated, the "assimilationist" tendency would have to be taken to its conclusion. This viewpoint is accompanied by a weariness of Judaism and a quite understandable wish to be free of the burdens of this affiliation. In the context of wholesale secularization, it is indeed hard to see how this sense of belonging might be grounded. If a person feels in no way constrained by the many obligations of the Torah, why should he forever be restrained by its "hedge"? If one does not experience the appeal of Zionism, if, moreover, one is alert to the ravages caused by nationalism in the last two centuries, what reason is there to claim an affiliation with a kind of nation? Nevertheless, if history teaches any lesson (understood in the most positive sense), it is that the Jewish identity continues to exist as a fact by the strangest pathways—even if its legitimacy is no longer perceived. Nothing has ever been able to erase this mark, not even the efforts of those who, having received it, no longer wanted it. Like it or not, the human race continues to be divided into Jews and Gentiles.

A second attitude, unfortunately, is rather widespread—in France at least. This attitude considers the Shoah to be absolutely unique and experiences indignation, as if before a profanation, in the face of any effort to compare it with other historical events. But in this understanding of the Shoah's uniqueness, only material circumstances are considered, to the exclusion of metaphysical or more precisely religious aspects: the gas chambers, death as an industry, the extermination of children, the plan to annihilate an entire people. These circumstances are indeed without parallel, and the Nazi extermination presents a unique picture. But every historical event, considered singly, is unique and nonrepeatable. Certain similar horrible elements are found in other contemporary exterminations, whereas others are not; and some elements that were absent from the Shoah are involved instead. All are unique, as is every child's death for its mother. That said, all children who die also have mothers.

The main disadvantage of this attitude is that it presents a false idea of Judaism. It is as if, contrary to the teaching of the Bible as well as the Talmud, one life were not as valuable as another, as if one crime were not equivalent to another one similarly defined. It suggests that the Jews exercise judgment according to two weights and two measures, that they inject a kind of "competition of victims" into historical consciousness; though all categories are equal, one victim is still "more equal" than the others. Of course, this attitude risks offending those peoples who have suffered as much—albeit differently. These peoples might be tempted to make Shylock's protestation their own: have we not feelings and passions like you? Do we not bleed when wounded, do we not die when we are killed? Are we not also human beings? "Fed with the same food, hurt with the same weapons . . . , warmed and cooled by the same winter and summer. . . ."

This, then, would be the upshot of the removal of religion from consideration: the implication that certain material considerations or moral qualities ground an *essential difference* between Jews and others. This viewpoint situates chosenness and privileges where they do not belong—where they cannot be recognized as legitimate. Further, it misrepresents the actual truth of chosenness and privileges. These are no longer understood as the free fruit and unique effect of the divine covenant on which they entirely depend—as Judaism has always taught.

The legitimacy of the Jews' claim to chosen status is recognized, in principle, outside the Jewish world. The Christian world, in spite of its mistakes, has always accepted the text that preceded it, the Old Testament, as valid and normative. But if an intellectual movement wishes to construe the essence of Judaism as something distinct from the particular relation that obtains between this people and the God of Abraham and Moses, then what meaning can the non-Jewish world attribute to the Shoah? For this same movement only affirms that it is meaningless, a pure negativity. From the outside, according to this view, the Shoah would seem to resemble a strange twin or shadow of Christianity. But here, the death of innocents—as a parallel to that of the Innocent—for which all of humanity is in a way at fault, would bear no power of redemption or reconciliation. To put a negative fact—the most negative fact imaginable, an absolute evil—at the center of consciousness without positing the final victory of the good is only to plant a gnawing pain there. The resulting inconsolable and vindictive distress would confront the whole world; since, again following the analogy with Christ, the whole world is guilty.

This would also deviate dangerously from Israel's particular calling, a sacerdotal calling in the service of our common humanity. There is a tradition in Judaism according to which the Jewish presence among the nations is a blessing to them. What would it mean if this presence came to represent a universal accusation?

Why is it that in France this movement—which surely is not as representative as it claims to be—is the loudest? Napoleon gave the Jews a common legal right to practice their religion and refused them any particular civic standing. Some French Jews left their religion but, despite their quasi-assimilation and their unquestioned patriotism, retained an instinct of "difference." Among these, there was a strong temptation to associate this difference with the murderous injustice to which the Nazis had subjected them on the one hand, and with the violation of their rights and their people's abandonment by the Vichy regime on the other. Later, in expanding circles, the scope of guilt by complicity was enlarged to infinity.

This temptation to associate difference with mistreatment has been reinforced by the secular climate of the French intellectual world. Having lost sight of theology, that world considers the Bible and the people that gave birth to it to be an element of our *culture* in a way identical to Greek philosophy and Roman law. As François Furet wrote in his correspondence with Ernst Nolte, "The Jewish people is inseparable from classical antiquity and from Christianity. . . . In martyring this people, in seeking to destroy it, the Nazis were killing European civilization."[3] This is very true, but it is not enough, even from the standpoint of a secularized history. After all, European culture developed on the basis of a lost Greece and fallen Rome; it did so while keeping the Jewish people—from whom the sacred book had come down—on the margins of what was said to be an exclusively Christian heritage. But the whole question lies in the meaning of this people long excluded, yet somehow still present.

Later, that people was "included" but deemed "unassimilable." The cultural approach does not resolve the mystery of Israel—no more, for that matter, than it solves the Christian mystery. From Sainte-Beuve through Renan to Maurras, this brilliant historiography surveys and praises the civilizing contribution of Christianity, while taking it as given that the question of its truth has been decided once and for all in the negative. One might ask whether Maurras's project of promoting a Catholicism without the Christian faith does not represent a kind of unconscious parallel to this lifeless Judaism—but is even further exacerbated by the loss of its living heart.

THE PAST HAS shown abundantly that Christian anti-Judaism tended to be harsher when it arose from social milieus that were ignorant of the fundamental tenets of their religion. The good Sancho Panza summed up his confession of faith in two points: veneration of the Holy Virgin and hatred of Jews. Once faith disappeared, anti-Semitism prospered more than ever, unchecked by the restraint that even this mutilated faith had applied. In the anti-Semitic literature of the prewar period, there could be no good Jew. Even the most sympathetic, the most virtuous carried, despite himself, a destructive virus inimical to Christians. All European history was reconstructed around a universal Jewish plot. During the year of the trial of Maurice Papon,[4] we heard remarks suggesting, for example, that anti-Semitism was just as virulent in de Gaulle's circle as it had been in Petain's; or that the essential axis of the history of France was hatred of Jews, from Saint Louis to the herding of Jews into the Paris Velodrome during the Second World War. I just read a novel which seems to say that there can be no "good goy," much less a good Christian: if one scratches the surface, the hateful anti-Semitic facilitator of the gas chamber bursts forth from the germ he contains. Such feelings are simply the reverse equivalent of yesterday's anti-Semitism. They stem, moreover, from milieus analogous to those that produced it. The same ignorance not only of the religion one confronts but also of one's own prevails, as does the same nationalistic exasperation that takes the place of religion. The risk, as Alain Finkielkraut wittily observed, is that opinion will be divided between "the overstimulated and the overwhelmed" (*les excités et les excédés*).

I do not want to push the comparison too far, since it would soon risk becoming unjust. Objectively, the Jews have suffered infinitely more at the hands of the Gentiles than the latter have from the former. Jewish anti-Christianity is more consistent with the Jewish faith than is the anti-Judaism of Christians; the latter, after all, immediately contradict their own faith by taking such a position. In a way, the Jewish anti-Christian attitude can be understood as the first step in a return to Zion following a century of secularization. While this impassioned opinion might be considered a way of fleeing true Judaism while remaining Jewish, it still remains faithful to one of its most fundamental precepts: that of never leaving the community.

Israel was built as a homeland to be shared by Jews, both by those faithful to the Law and by those liberated from it but wanting to live freely and in safety. What those who came from Europe had most in common was the fact that, together, they had been the object of an attempted annihilation. This is why the Shoah was invoked as a rallying point: both as a principle of legitimacy for all peoples who had a share of responsibility, and for those Jews who were distant from the Torah and for whom biblical legitimacy had become a remote principle. Still, a "religion of the Shoah" could neither combine with nor substitute for biblical religion without committing idolatry and aggravating the enmity between the Jews and the nations the hedge of the Torah does not command.

A third position consists in reflecting on the Shoah by pondering the bond between the Jewish people and the God of its fathers. A conviction of faith cannot be put aside: the Jewish people have suffered for the cause of God. Since the time of the covenant, this has been the weight and price of election. In the face of the distilled idolatry and blasphemy of Nazism, this people struggled and testified for the honor of the Name. And yet it is impossible to measure the scandal represented by this event and the difficulty of conceptualizing it theologically.

The Jewish people exists solely as the partner to a covenant with a God who has bound himself by promises: "For the Lord's portion is his people; Jacob is the lot of his inheritance. He found him in a desert land, and in the wasteland howling wilderness; He led him about, He instructed him, He kept him as the apple of His eye. As an eagle stirs up her nest, flutters over her young, spreads abroad her wings, takes them, bears them on her wings" (Deut. 32:11). There are twenty more texts like this one in the Bible. Precisely that part of the people that believed these promises most fervently—the pious communities of Central and Eastern Europe—was hit hardest by the catastrophe. The relatively unbelieving part was spared the most: those who dared before the war, against the opinion of most rabbis, to conceive of and achieve the Zionist utopia. And during the war, it was the most faithless part—by this time lodged within the most fanatical communism—that fought effectively against the Nazi machine.

Judaism does not share the familiarity with evil, the recognition of the permanence and recurrence of evil that the dogma of original sin introduced into the Christian world. In its Pauline form, this dogma has not been accepted by Israel's Wise Men, no more than they have accepted the dialectic of sin and grace, the possible victory of evil, and the certain victory—in hope—of good. The Jewish author of the Syriac Apocalypse ascribed to Baruch explicitly rejects original sin: "Adam was cause only for himself, and each of us has become the Adam of his own life."[5] Why, then, have the righteous—and especially the righteous—perished?

In the Shoah, each individual died alone, as a unique person. We know that many prayed before the "silence of God." Many kept and even rediscovered the faith. Many too were those who lost it. Theological reflection on the Shoah has been as intense as it has been

85

diverse. Some rabbis attribute to it an essential resemblance with the other catastrophes that have struck Israel since ancient times; others deny this resemblance. Some meditate on the mysterious aporias of the book of Job; still others relate the Shoah mysteriously to the rise of Israel on the Land of Promise. Emil Fackenheim seems to lean towards a theology of the "death of God." Hans Jonas, the great specialist on gnosticism, proposes (somewhat half-heartedly, it seems to me) a gnostic myth of the impotence and withdrawal of God from the affairs of this world. Let us allow this reflection to develop: it is not yet neared its conclusion or any agreement. This work of theological elaboration, whatever its final form may be, will probably be the force that will overcome the contradictions and difficulties of the first two attitudes. This in turn will satisfy the mind not only of the philosopher and the theologian, but also of the historian anxious not to neglect any facts.

CHRISTIAN MEMORY OF NAZISM

While reflection on communism remains very marginal in the Christian consciousness, the memory of Nazism exercises and troubles it, producing very significant effects.

Whereas Christianity was predisposed toward communism by socialist humanitarianism, it was driven towards fascism—and, in Germany, towards Nazism—by a neighboring branch of the same romantic trunk: the communitarian and organicist ideals that were gradually transformed into the "ethnic" ideal. Cardinal Faulhaber, the archbishop of Berlin who otherwise tenaciously resisted Hitler, imprudently remarked in a 1933 homily that the church "had no objection to efforts to conserve as purely as possible the national characteristics of a people, nor to stimulating its national spirit by emphasizing the blood ties that consecrate its unity." He had no idea of the sinister echo of these words he would hear before long.

The Christian churches in Germany resisted unevenly. A minority gave itself over completely to the "German Christian" tendency, which was more Protestant than Catholic. A greater number sought to salvage what they could, to placate the regime and protect people—with modest success. Finally, a smaller number—as is reasonable to expect in all totalitarian regimes—protested and opposed the regime, thus risking and sometimes sacrificing their lives.

Once the Nazi regime was destroyed, there was no amnesty. Criminals were judged and condemned. All of Germany was forced to make a gigantic examination of conscience, invited to reject whatever in its history and thought might have paved the way for the disaster. This was done at the cost of a certain evacuation of the German soul and an eclipse of its creative capacity. The manner in which this people—ruined, decimated, bisected, and dishonored—resisted despair and returned to work, accepting its punishment, is worthy of admiration. The rapid recovery of Germany after 1945 and the long stagnation of Russia after 1991 are not unrelated to the humility of the one, finally recovered, and the pride of the other.

Nazism massacred many Christians. In Poland alone, it was three million—as many as the massacred Jews. It was determined to destroy the church in due time. Nevertheless, the fact remains that the Christian memory of Nazism focuses not on the general massacre or on the persecutions of the church, but very specifically on the fate of the Jews and the responsibility of the church as a whole for the events related to the Final Solution.

Having been sharply attacked on this point, the Catholic Church has made its case. Father Pierre Blet S.J., a historian of competence recognized by his peers, recently gathered the Catholic arguments in a work supported by documents from the Vatican archives.[6] Of all the public bodies that fell under Nazi domination, he argues, the church saved the most Jews. Father Blet estimates their number at 800,000. The encyclical *Mit Brennender Sorge* (March 1937) expressly condemned racism as well as the various racial idolatries of blood or the nation. The silence for which Pius XII has been reproached can be explained by prudence and by his concern to maximize effectiveness.[7] He sought, for example, to avoid provoking still more murderous Nazi reprisals, such as those that occurred in the Netherlands after the bishops protested, and to preserve a portion of the ecclesiastical structure and diplomatic network. It was hoped that this would allow for at least weak action in Germany on the basis of the concordat, and stronger action in the satellite countries that had not yet been occupied (such as Hungary or Slovakia). Pius XII also sought to avoid systematically weakening Germany in the face of the Soviet menace—which the pope rightly considered to be a more dangerous menace to humanity than Nazism in the long term. His silence can also be explained by how difficult it was to believe the reports of the great Nazi secret when they first began to filter through; for Pius XII, as for the Allied leaders, such reports were simply unbelievable. This defense put forward by Father Blet must be given careful attention. Still, it leaves two points unresolved.

First, it was clear from the style of the church's action on behalf of the Jews that it regarded them as victims it must aid by virtue of a *general* duty of humanity and charity. It felt as foreign to them as they to it, and it accepted this symmetry. It did not consider that Nazism, by attacking the Jewish people, was attacking Christianity at its still-living root. When it attacked both Jews and the church, these were not two different crimes, two acts of sacrilege, but in fact one and the same. The famous silence of Pius XII was not as absolute as is said. But whatever its prudential, perhaps justifiable motives (and who can say a half century later?), it takes on a color more dramatic than the silence of the political leaders of the alliance. These, even if they wanted to protect the Jews, considered them foreign nationals. Unlike the later John Paul II, Pius XII did not hold the Jews to be "elder brothers" in a single faith.

Pius XI strongly condemned theoretical Marcionism in the 1937 encyclical, although he did not judge it opportune to mention the ancient heresy by name. But neither did he mention the Jews or pronounce their name. This silence seems to me still more striking than that of Pius XII, since Pius XI was free in Rome, in a state that was still sovereign. Yet his theoretical condemnation did not prevent the drift in practice of later years. More precisely, the Nazi crime brutally brought to light the germ of Marcionism that lay hidden and enveloped in the ordinary theology of the church and suffused the relationship between Jews and Christians. The Jews are the subsisting relic, the witness of Israel *vetus*, an Israel henceforth obsolete and dispossessed of its heritage, which had fallen altogether into the hands of Israel *verus*. Thus, the sole relationship with Christians the Jews retain is that of an ambivalent archeological memory. Meritorious for having prepared the coming of Christ, they are guilty for not having recognized him and having crucified him. One owed them, therefore, only a general but equivocal charity: other strangers to the church deserved neither this praise nor this blame. The Christian attitude during the war was modeled on this equivocation, leaning sometimes one way and sometimes the other.

The second point is the following: under the influence of this theological estrangement from the Jewish people, the Catholic Church, or at least its personnel, was vulnerable to the inebriating effects of the ideological lie.

The first misstep was to enter into a concordat with Hitler's regime. This resulted from a failure of political analysis. The Nazi regime was taken to be an extreme form of the authoritarian, despotic, or tyrannical regime—a rich collection of which the church had already encountered in its long history. It did not recognize the absolute novelty of Nazism early enough, even in relation to Italian fascism, with which it had signed a legitimate concordat that guaranteed it a provisional *modus vivendi*. The concordat with Hitler bound the church without binding the Nazi regime. The church was confined to an exaggerated moderation by the fear of losing the last shreds of a treaty that was being torn up day by day.

The second misstep, which followed from the first, was graver still: the church felt itself compelled to take the worldview imposed by Nazism seriously. In the documents of the nunciatures, it is as though the reality of the "racial problem" and the distinction between Aryans and non-Aryans were taken for granted.

Here, a general rule applies. When one is contending with an ideological regime, the line that must be held absolutely to the end is to reject, without discussion, the description of reality set forth by this regime. As soon as one puts one's finger in the gears and admits this description includes a "partial truth"—for example, that there are Aryans and non-Aryans, and that a "Jewish problem" therefore exists—one is lost. The will now obeys only a distorted intelligence. It remains only to beg the "Aryans" to resolve this "problem" in a "humane" manner. In the world of ideology, the "partial truth" that holds seductive power is the very site of falsification and what is most false. This rule holds true for all ideology, and particularly for communist ideology. As soon as people accepted a description that divided reality between socialism and capitalism, they could only beg the two "camps" to obey the general principles of morality— even if this meant granting superiority, in principle, to the first for its having done away with "exploitation."

The *No*, the refusal to discuss, must be set forth from the first moment. If it is not, one loses one's sense of the false logic that occurs with the second step, which is introduced by *therefore*. The Treaty of Versailles humiliated Germany: *therefore* it is necessary to take a certain measure in order to solve the Jewish problem, *therefore*. . . . Until, by an imperceptible drift, one arrives at the Final Solution. Workers are exploited: *therefore* there must be a revolution, *therefore* . . . etc. We must flee the "partial truth," because this truth, however indisputable in appearance, is already embedded in a system of insane logic.

Assuming we have now attained the historical distance necessary to measure intellectual resistance to Nazism and communism, one might judge that the resistance of Christians who remained Christian and exempt from all temptation and compromise of principle on this matter was grounded more in moral rectitude than in intellectual lucidity. Among the analysts of the period extending from, let us say, 1935 to 1950, one finds few Christian thinkers among those who were most acute—Orwell, Koestler, Souvarine, Aron. To be sure, one can point to a Maritain, a Journet, a Gaston Fessard, or a Karl Barth (though this latter only on the subject of Nazism). In the security of their theology, these found the resources to enlighten their discernment. Among too many others, though, the good use of reason was hindered by religious instincts. Faith and charity remained intact, but they were paralyzed by doctrinal impurities issuing from upstream, by timidity, and by a dearth of intellectual labor.

But whereas communist intimidation would delay any examination of conscience for decades (in fact such examination has still not really begun), the complete defeat of Nazism and the public enormity of its crimes would trigger in the church a moral and theological awareness of this event from the first years after the war.

Cardinal Ratzinger declared in 1996: "It is important to note that the Holocaust was committed not by Christians in the name of Christ, but by anti-Christians, and as the preparatory phase to the extermination of Christianity." He adds, however, the following:

> But this in no way changes the fact that people who had been baptized were responsible. Even though the SS was an organization of atheist criminals, and there were hardly any Christians among them, it still remains that they had been baptized. Christian anti-Semitism had prepared the ground up to a certain point; this cannot be denied. . . . This is something that should move us to a constant examination of our conscience.[8]

A remarkable point of this declaration is the seriousness with which it considers the sacrament of baptism. The cardinal does not esteem that the criminals' abandonment of the faith and of the Christian religion freed them from being Christian. Their apostasy in no way erases their baptism. The church, to which they still belong objectively to some degree, is not free of responsibility. Since we take notice of the Jewishness of an individual who does not identify himself as Jewish (in communism, for example), we should likewise acknowledge the Christian background of a baptized apostate.

The church has referred this responsibility mainly to its teaching. A Roman Catholic document of 1998 acknowledges that the anti-Jewish content of the church's oldest tradition prepared the ground for a racist anti-Semitism that is in fact foreign to the church. This seems to me to be the right way to frame the issue. The church is not as seriously responsible for the sins of its members as for the teaching it gave them—a teaching that did not sufficiently prepare them to resist the malignant solicitations of certain historical circumstances. The function of teaching governs all other activities of the church. Such men as the great rabbis Jacob Kaplan and Jules Isaac do the church a great service by sharply calling it to account on this point. And such demands have in fact been satisfied, from the Seelisberg Conference of 1947 to Vatican II and beyond. The "teaching of contempt" no longer has currency.

But the examination of conscience did not stop there. Little by little, the question of the church's relationship with the Jews—first envisioned as a matter of reestablishing peace with an external partner—was deepened to include the church's relationship with itself. Thus, it was its own tradition that had to be examined, as well as its own interpretation of the Scriptures. Within the penumbra surrounding the question of the status of Jews and Judaism after the coming of the Messiah, it was discovered that teachings had proliferated that were either false or inadequate; and these teachings had produced unacceptable consequences in our time. The ramifications of this discovery reached far in all directions within the patrimony of the church and brought about a general rebalancing. This process is not finished. It may yet result in a theological event as important as the councils of Nicaea and Chalcedon were in their times.

THE UNIQUENESS OF THE SHOAH

The lengthy discussions and analyses that make up this essay have been necessary—though no doubt insufficient—to provide the beginning of a response to the question posed at the outset: how should we understand the uniqueness of the Shoah?

The labor of Christian memory concerning Nazism in its immediately theological aspect arrives naturally at an acknowledgment of the uniqueness of the Shoah.

During the war and even afterwards, there were voices that interpreted the catastrophe that befell the Jews as a confirmation of the curse attached to a "deicide" people. It would be hard to be more abject. But from the moment one ceased to impute to Israel the sin of "deicide" (absurd, and already refuted by the catechism of Trent), another figure came to the fore: the suffering servant of the book of Isaiah, a figure in whom the Jews had always seen Israel, and Christians, Christ. Henceforth, the analogy of the two figures was interpreted in order to honor the Chosen People. It also justified the uniqueness of the Shoah by taking into consideration a single criterion: the unique character of the victim. This theological point of view dissipated all possible confusion of it with a simple massacre; within the massive slaughter of the era, the Shoah was set apart and carried a different meaning.

There was nothing so banal in the Roman empire as the torture of crucifixion. Following Spartacus's rebellion, crosses lined the Appian Way from Rome to Campania. The Jewish Wars of Titus and of Hadrian eventually saw the erection of thousands of crosses. The Jews themselves sometimes used this means of execution, in cases when they enjoyed enough sovereignty to have the right to it. Thus, according to Josephus, King Alexander Jannaeus had eight hundred Jews crucified in the very center of Jerusalem. The Messiah was put on a cross between two men who, according to the Gospel, suffered longer than him—it was necessary to break their legs so that they would die before the Sabbath. Nonetheless, Christians believe that the Passion cannot be compared with these routine executions. However horrible men's agony may be, it gives no idea of the reality of the passion of a God become man; the extent of this passion can be measured only in relation to the divine plan of creation. By analogy, the same incommensurability sets apart the people who have received election, who remain an instrument in this plan, and to whom the Messiah belongs.

Christians are thus in possession of a coherent theological scheme of the Shoah—one that does justice at once to the Jewish sense of difference and to the peoples, Christian or otherwise, who have undergone comparable trials. There can be no "competition of victims" among such peoples. Without either confusion or separation, they rank equally in the choir of innocent sufferers and are united in the solidarity of a theological order that remains to be wholly defined.

In effect, what appears to Christians as a moment of agony in the long labor of redemption obviously appears to Jews as a pure scandal. Certain Jews rejected the word "holocaust" because it indicated a sacrifice: they thought it was not appropriate for naming this senseless paroxysm of evil and preferred the neutral term "Shoah," or "catastrophe," instead. Christians could accept the term Holocaust because it had been lived and recapitulated by their Messiah precisely as a sacrifice. The mutual misunderstanding on this subject, therefore, is based neither on a simple mistake nor on ill will; it arises instead from the very roots of the Jewish and Christian faiths. Christians believe they possess a key to understanding within the limits of what is knowable. But this key functions only within the limits of their faith. It is rejected by Jews, and Christians fail to understand this rejection. Thus, the problem of the uniqueness of the Shoah admits of no universal solution. We are left simply to understand this unresolved problem clearly, and to accept it.

APPENDIX
THE MEMORY AND OBLIVION OF BOLSHEVISM[1]

TODAY THERE IS a fairly general agreement—at least among members of the Institut de France—concerning the degree of kinship between communism of the Bolshevik type and National Socialism. I find Pierre Chaunu's expression felicitous: heterozygous twins. These two ideologies took power in the twentieth century. Their goal was to achieve a perfect society by removing the evil principle that constituted an obstacle. In one case, the evil principle was property, and therefore, property-holders. But because evil persisted after the "liquidation as a class" of this group, the target became all those corrupted by the spirit of "capitalism," which had infiltrated the Communist Party itself. In the second case, the evil principle was located within races said to be "inferior" and, above all, within the Jews. But then, because evil continued to exist after their extermination, it had to be hunted down in the other races and in the "Aryan race" itself, since its "purity" had been polluted. Communism and Nazism invoked the authority of science to ground their legitimacy. They proposed to reeducate humanity and to create a new man.

These two ideologies considered themselves philanthropic. National Socialism sought the good of the German people and claimed to render a service to humanity by exterminating the Jews. Leninist communism directly sought the good of all humanity. The universalism of communism gave it a great advantage over Nazism, whose program cannot be exported. The two doctrines proposed "elevated ideals" fit to elicit enthusiastic devotion and heroic acts. But they also dictated the right and the duty to kill. To quote Chateaubriand, who in this case was prophetic: "At the bottom of these diverse systems lies a heroic remedy, whether avowed or implied: this remedy is to kill." And Hugo: "You can kill this man in good conscience"—or even whole categories of men. And this is just what these doctrines did when they gained access to power on a scale unknown in history. This is why, in the eyes of those outside their systems, Nazism and communism are criminal. But are they equally criminal? Having studied both, I am familiar with the summits of intensity in the crimes of Nazism (the gas chamber) and extensiveness in those of communism (more than sixty million dead), as well as with the perversion of souls and minds effected by both. Thus, I believe there is no point in entering this dangerous discussion. We must respond very simply and firmly: yes, they are equally criminal.

The question for us is the following: how is it that today historical memory treats the two ideologies unequally to the point of seeming to forget communism? There is no need to go on at length about the fact of this disparity. Already in 1989, the Polish opposition, led by authorities of the church, recommended forgetting and forgiveness. In most countries leaving communism behind, there has been no question of punishing those responsible for killing their subjects, for depriving them of their freedom or ruining and brutalizing them—and this for two or three generations. Indeed, except in East Germany and the Czech Republic, communists were permitted to remain in the political game; and this allowed them in some cases to retake power. In Russia and other republics, diplomatic and police personnel remained in place. In the West, this de facto amnesty was well received: retention of the *nomenklatura* was compared to the Thermidoran evolution of former Jacobins. For some time, our media have spoken casually of a "communist epic." The past links of the Communist Party with the Comintern have been duly exposed and documented, but this does not prevent its having been accepted in the heart of French democracy.

On the other hand, the *damnatio memoriae* of Nazism, far from being subject to the slightest limitation, seems to grow worse every day. Every year more volumes are added to an already ample library. Museums and expositions rightly maintain our sense of the horror of the crime.

Let us run a search in the records of a major evening newspaper. Using key words and covering the years 1990 till the day of the search—June 14, 1997—we find that "Nazism" occurs 480 times, "Stalinism," 7; "Auschwitz," 105; "Kolyma," 2; "Magadan," 1; "Kouropaty," 0; "Ukrainian famine" (five to six million died in 1933), 0. This survey has suggestive value.

On the subject of his book *La Mémoire et l'Oubli* [Memory and Oblivion], Alfred Grosser stated the following in 1989: "All I ask, when one weighs responsibility for past crimes, is that the same criteria be applied to everyone." Of course this is right, but it is very difficult to achieve. I wish here to attempt, as a simple historian and not as a judge, to interpret these facts *sine ira et studio*. There is no way I can exhaust the subject, but I can perhaps draw up a nonexclusive list of factors:

1) Nazism is better known than communism because the closet of corpses was opened wide by the Allied troops and because several Western European peoples experienced it directly. I have often asked student audiences whether they have any knowledge of the artificial famine organized in Ukraine in 1933. They have not heard of it. Nazi crime was mainly physical; it did not morally contaminate its

victims and witnesses, who were not required to adhere to Nazism. It is therefore easy to spot, flagrant. The gas chamber, conceived in order to exterminate a definite portion of humanity with industrial efficiency, is a unique fact. The gulag and the *Laogai* remain enveloped in a fog, like a distant object known only indirectly. Cambodia is an exception: its mass graves are now being uncovered.

2) The Jewish people have taken charge of the memory of the Shoah. For them, this was a moral obligation inscribed in the long memory of persecutions: a religious obligation linked to praise and impassioned questioning of the Lord in the manner of Job. For had the Lord not promised to protect his people and punish injustice and crime?

3) Nazism and communism have been caught up in the magnetic field constituted by a polarity between the notions of right and left. This is a complex phenomenon. On the one hand, the idea of the left accompanies the entry of successive social classes into the play of democratic politics. But it must be noted that promotion of the American working class has excluded the socialist idea, and that a majority of the English, German, Scandinavian, and Spanish working class have rejected the communist idea—even though their power has increased. Only in France, in Czechoslovakia immediately after the war, and later in Italy was communism able to identify itself with the workers' movement and become a rightful member of the left. It should also be noted that, in France, historians such as Mathiez (who admired the Great Revolution) quite naturally drew a parallel between October 1917 and 1792 and between the Bolshevik and the Jacobin terrors.

In addition, many historians of the prewar period were keenly aware of the socialist or proletarian roots of Italian fascism and German Nazism. As evidence I cite Elie Halévy's classic, *History of European Socialism*, written in 1937. The third chapter of the fifth part is devoted to the socialism of fascist Italy, the fourth chapter, to that of National Socialism. The latter regime, by declaring itself anticapitalist, dispossessing or eliminating traditional elites, and taking on a revolutionary form, could well have claimed a role in the history of socialism. But today, Halévy's suggestion would be inconceivable.

4) By creating a military alliance between the democracies and the Soviet Union, the Second World War weakened the West's defenses against the communist idea—defenses that had still been very strong at the time of the Hitler-Stalin pact. This provoked a kind of intellectual paralysis. In order to maintain the will to conduct a war, a democracy needs its ally to have a certain degree of respectability; if necessary, it confers such respectability. With Stalin's encouragement, Soviet military heroism took a purely patriotic form, and communist ideology was held in reserve, hidden. Unlike Eastern Europe, Western Europe had no direct experience of the arrival of the Red Army. Thus, it was seen as a liberator in the same way the Allied armies were, although this was not the experience of the Baltic peoples or the Poles. Soviets were judges at Nuremberg. Democracies agreed to some very heavy sacrifices in order to defeat the Nazi regime. Later, they agreed only to lighter sacrifices in order to contain the Soviet regime—even, toward the end, to help it endure, out of concern for stability. That regime crumbled upon its own nothingness all on its own, without much help from the democracies. Thus, there is no way the attitude of Westerners could be the same in this case as it has been toward the Nazis, nor could their judgment be equal or their memory impartial.

5) One of the great successes of the Soviet regime is that it diffused and, little by little, imposed its own ideological classification of modern political regimes. Lenin saw everything in terms of the opposition between "socialism" and "capitalism." Up into the '30s, Stalin preserved this dichotomy. Capitalism, also known as "imperialism," encompassed not only liberal regimes, but also social-democratic, fascist, and National Socialist ones. This made it possible for German communists to hold the "social-fascists" and Nazis in equal balance. However, in determining the politics of so-called popular fronts, the following classification emerged:

"socialism" (that is, the Soviet regime), "bourgeois democracies" (liberal and social-democratic regimes), and finally, "fascism." Under fascism, the following regimes were lumped together: Nazism, Mussolini's fascism, the very authoritarian regimes that dominated in Spain, Portugal, Austria, Hungary, Poland, etc., and finally, the extreme right of liberal regimes. Thus, a continuous chain ran from Jean Chiappe[2] to Hitler, passing through Franco, Mussolini, etc. The specific character of Nazism was thereby effaced. It was also firmly located on the right, over which it projected its black light. It became the absolute right, whereas Soviet communism was the absolute left.

What is surprising is that, in a country like France, this classification became fixed in the historical consciousness. Consider the texts used in our secondary and higher education. The classification is generally the following: the Soviet regime, liberal democracies, with their left and right parties, then the various forms of fascism—Nazism, Italian, Spanish Francoism, etc. This is an attenuated version of the Soviet vulgate. One rarely finds the correct classification in these textbooks, the one Hannah Arendt proposed as early as 1951 and upon which contemporary historians agree. That second classification is the following: in one category, there are two *totalitarian* regimes, communism and Nazism, then the liberal regimes, then the authoritarian ones (Italy, Spain, Hungary, Latin America)—with this last based on the classical categories of dictatorship and tyranny as identified by Aristotle.

6) Another factor is the weakness of groups that would have been capable of preserving the memory of communism. Nazism lasted twelve years; European communism, depending on the country, endured for between fifty and seventy years. This duration, in effect, allowed communism to grant itself amnesty. During this very long period, civil society was atomized, elites were successively destroyed, replaced, and reeducated. From top to bottom, almost everyone was involved in trafficking, betrayal, and moral degradation. Graver still, most of those who might have been able to think were

deprived of the knowledge of their history and lost their capacity to analyze. Reading the literature of Russian opposition—the only true literature of the country—we hear a heartbreaking plea, the touching expression of infinite distress, but rarely does one find rational analysis. The consciousness of communism is painful, but it remains confused. Today, young Russian historians have little interest in studying this disgusting period destined to oblivion. In any case, the state is again closing up the archives. The only milieu that might have carried on a lucid memory of communism is that of the dissidents born around 1970. But this group disintegrated rapidly in 1991 and has not been able to participate in the new government. This is why its attempt at *memorial* did not take root and develop. For it would be necessary, in effect, that the organ whose function it is to remember would attain a certain critical mass in terms of numbers, power, and influence. The Armenians have never quite reached this critical mass. Still less have the Ukrainians, the Kazaks, the Chechnyans, the Tibetans, and too many others to mention.

Nothing is so problematic after the dissolution of a totalitarian regime as the reconstitution of the people's normal moral conscience and intellectual capacity. In this respect, post-Nazi Germany found itself in a better situation than post-Soviet Russia. Civil society did not have the time to be destroyed in depth. Judged, punished, and de-Nazified by Western armies, West Germany was able to continue with this purifying movement, to judge itself, remember, and repent.

Things were different in Eastern Europe, and the West is partly responsible for this. When the communists transformed their possession of goods into legitimate property, when they legitimized their de facto power by universal suffrage, when they replaced Leninism with the most chauvinist nationalism, the West found it inopportune to call them to account. This was the worst disservice they could render Russia. The ubiquity of statues of Lenin in Russian public places is but the visible sign of a poisoning of souls, the cure of which will take years. And in the West, the historical vulgate left by the Komintern of popular fronts is far from being erased. The inclusion of the Leninist idea in the idea of the left would have horrified Karl Kautsky, Eduard Bemstein, Léon Blum, Bertrand Russell, and even Rosa Luxemburg. Nonetheless, it means that Leninism is sometimes likened to an unfortunate mishap, a kind of meteorological accident affecting this broader left. Now that it is gone, the idea lives on as a kind of honorable project that turned out badly.

7) The amnesia concerning communism and the memory of Nazism are mutually exasperating, whereas a simple and just memory suffices to condemn them both. For centuries, the Western bad conscience has insisted that it must be the home of absolute evil. Opinions have varied on the precise location: evil has sometimes been situated in South African apartheid, or in America's Vietnam War, but it has always centered on Nazi Germany. Russia, Korea, China, and Cuba were experienced as external, or pushed to the outside to the degree that people preferred to turn their eyes away. The vague remorse that has accompanied this neglect has been compensated by vigilance, a ferocious concentration of attention on everything that had anything to do with Nazism, on the Vichy regime, or, today, on the perverse ideas secreted in certain cells of Europe's extreme right.

IT IS CHARACTERISTIC of the twentieth century that its history was not only horrible in terms of human massacres, but that historical awareness—and this explains the former point—has had particular difficulty finding a true orientation. Orwell remarked that many became Nazis through an understandable horror of Bolshevism, and communists through an understandable horror of Nazism. This points out the danger of historical falsifications. But we can see one about to take shape now, and it would be a pity to bequeath a falsified history to the coming century.

In concluding, I mention one hope and one fear. Because it exceeded what was believed possible, it took years to grasp Nazism completely. Human imagination fell short. The same might happen concerning Bolshevik communism, the works of which have opened up an abyss just as deep. These works have been protected—as Auschwitz was until 1945—by being improbable, unbelievable, and unthinkable. Time, whose function is to reveal the truth, will perhaps perform its office in this case as well.

NOTES

INTRODUCTION

1. Taken from a speech delivered at the Institut de France in October 1997. A transcript of the speech can be found in the appendix. It was simultaneously published in *Commentaire* (No. 80, 1997–98) and *Commentary* (January 1998). The latter was published in New York under the auspices of the American Jewish Committee. Both journals published readers' reactions in the following issue.

CHAPTER ONE

1. Raul Hilberg, *The Destruction of the European Jews* (New York: Holmes & Meier, 1985).
2. Vladimir Zazoubrine, *Le Tchékiste* (Paris: Christian Bourgois, 1990).

CHAPTER TWO

1. Heinrich Himmler, *Discours secrets* (Paris: Gallimard, 1978).

2. Tragedy understood as the pervasive principle of reality. *[trans.]*
3. Raymond Aron, *Démocratie et totalitarisme* (Paris: Gallimard, 1965), 302.
4. Ibid.

CHAPTER THREE

1. Sebastien Haffner, *Un certain Adolf Hitler* (Paris: Grasset, 1979), 242.
2. Immanuel Kant, *Critique de la faculté de juger* (Paris: Vrin, 1969), § 46.

CHAPTER FOUR

1. G. W. F. Hegel, *L'Esprit du christianisme et son destin* (Paris: Vrin, 1971), 6–26 passim.
2. Adolph Harnack, *L'Essence du christianisme* (Paris: Librairie Fischbacher, 1907).
3. Hermann Rauschning, *Hitler m'a dit* (Paris: Coopération,1939), 269.

CHAPTER FIVE

1. Anne Applebaum, *New Criterion* 115, no. 2 (October 1996).
2. Annie Kriegel, "L'antisémitisme de Staline," *Les Nour veaux Cahiers,* no. 120, 1995, 55.
3. *Commentaire,* no. 80, 1997–98, 805.
4. In 1998, for ordering the deportation of French Jews to Germany. *[trans.]*
5. Cited by Ephraïm Urbach, *Les Sages d'Israël* (Paris: Cerf-Verdier, 1996), 440.
6. Pierre Blet S.J., *Pie XII et la Seconde Guerre mondiale d'après les archives du Vatican* (Paris: Perrin, 1997).
7. This silence was not absolute. In his radio message of Christmas 1942, Pius XII declared: "Humanity owes this wish [to bring society to the unshakable center of gravity of divine law in the service of the human person and of the community ennobled by God] to the hundreds of millions of people who, through no fault of their own, and sometimes for no reason but their nationality or race, have been consigned to death or to progressive extermination." In a speech delivered to the college of cardinals on June 2,

1943, he declared: "Every word we address on this subject to the competent authorities, every public allusion, we must seriously consider and measure in the interest of the very ones who suffer, in order not to render their situation grave and unbearable despite our best intentions." This alludes to the denunciation of persecution by the Dutch episcopacy in July 1942, which was followed by roundups of Jews and reprisals against baptized Jews. The pope adds, "The Vicar of Christ, even though he asked for nothing more than pity and a sincere return to the elementary laws of right and humanity, often found himself before doors than no key could open."

8. Cardinal Ratzinger, *Le Sel de la terre* (Paris: Flammarion-Cerf, 1997), 242.

APPENDIX

1. Speech delivered at the Institut de France for the annual public meeting of the five academies, October 21, 1997.
2. The right-wing police prefect whose dismissal in 1934 provoked massive demonstrations.

INDEX

Abraham, 61, 62, 67, 81
Adam, 85
aesthetics, 21, 24, 47
Africa, 26, 51
Akhmatova, Anna, 53, 58
Albania, 56
Alexander Jannaeus, 93
American Jewish Committee, 105n1
Anabaptists, 69
anti-Semitism, 16
    Catholic Church and, 92
    Christianity and, 83–86
    in France, 83
    of Hitler, Adolf, 63
    Nazi "biblicism" and, 61–63
appeasement, 43
Applebaum, Anne, 79
Aragon, Louis, 15
Arcadia, 42
Arendt, Hannah, xix, 24, 79, 100
Armenians, 78, 101

Aron, Raymond, xix, 27–29, 42,
    79, 91
Aryans, 3, 42
Asia, 4, 6, 35, 51
Assyrian conquest, xviii
atheism
    communism and, 67
    of Hitler, Adolf, 63
Aufhebung, 42
Augustine, Saint, 59
Auschwitz, xvi, xvii, 1, 6, 37, 102
Avars, 77

Babylonian conquest, xviii
Bakunin, Mikhail, 25, 47
baptism, 91–92
Barth, Karl, 91
Baruch, 85
Battle of the Bulge, 44
Belzec, 1

Bemstein, Eduard, 102
Benedict XVI, Pope, 91
Bible, 80, 82
    morality and, 26
    salvation and, 59, 60
Black Book of Communism, The, xiv,
    10, 37
Blet, Pierre, 87, 88
Bloy, Léon, 63
Blum, Léon, 102
Boethius, 57
Bolshevik Party, 39, 75
Bolshevism
    Judaism and, 44
    maxim of, 25
    memory of, 95–103
    moral imperative underlying,
      24
    prehistory of, 24, 25
    See also communism
Brecht, Bertolt, 15
Brezhnev, Leonid, 50, 51
Buber-Neumann, Margarete, xx
Buchenwald, xvi
Bukharin, Nikolai, 42
Bukovsky, 7
Bulgakov, Mikhail, 58

Cambodia, xxi, 5, 31, 78, 98
capitalism
    communism and, 28, 30
    Lenin, Vladimir and, 30–31
    socialism and, 90
Catholic Church
    anti-Semitism and, 92
    baptism and, 91–92
    Jewishness, religious
      consciousness of and,
      xviii

    Nazism, Christian memory of
      and, 87–92
Caucasus, 4
Ceausescus, 56
Cerinthus, 66
Chalcedon, Council of, 92
Chamberlain, Neville, 43
Chateaubriand, 96
Chaunu, Pierre, xiii, 95
Chechens, 5, 101
Chelmno, 1
Chiappe, Jean, 100
China, 7, 26, 31, 35, 50, 71–72, 78
    Cultural Revolution in, 5,
      16, 48
    famine and, 9
    Great Leap Forward in, 5, 48
    mobile slaughter operations
      in, 5
Christ, 82, 89, 93–94
Christianity
    anti-Semitism and, 83–86
    apostasy and, 74, 91–92
    "biblicism," communist and,
      64–66
    "biblicism," Nazi and, 61–64
    communism and, 72–74, 86
    evil and, 73, 85
    forgetting and forgiveness and,
      73–74
    German, 86–87
    heresies and, 66–69
    humanitarianism and, 65, 86
    Jews and, 69, 83, 87–92
    Nazism and, 17–18, 86–92
    salvation and, 72
    sin and, 73, 85
Church Fathers, xviii
Cold War, 51
Comintern, 48, 97, 102

Commentaire, 105n1
Commentary, 105n1
communism
    apostasy, Christian and, 74,
        91–92
    atheism and, 67
    "biblicism" of, 64–66
    Bolshevik, xiv–xx
    capitalism and, 28, 30
    Christian memory of, 86
    definition of, 2
    evil and, 54, 76
    gnosticism and, 68
    goal of, xiii, 46–48, 95
    good, falsification of and,
        24–26, 29
    historical memory of, xiii–xiv
    humanitarianism and, 86
    ideology of, xv, 25, 28
    intellectual geneology of,
        13–17
    Jewish memory of, 75
    judicial execution and, 8–9
    Leninist, xiii, 29–30, 96
    liberty and, 26, 27
    memory of, 71–75, 86, 100–
        101, 102
    moral destruction and, 13–17,
        21, 24–26, 31, 32–36
    morality of, 21, 24–26, 26–30
    National Socialism and,
        95–96
    "pagan" oblivion of, 71–72
    as philanthropic, xiii, 96
    physical destruction and, 1–11
    political life, destruction of
        and, 39–40, 41–42,
        46–48, 48–51
    power and, xv, 31–32, 49,
        57–58
    progress and, 24–25, 42
    right and left, struggle
        between and, 98–99
    right to kill and, xiii
    salvation and, 58–59, 69
    science and, 95–96
    universalism and, 21, 30
    universalism of, 96
Communist Party, 41, 76
concentration, 3–4
containment, 51
Cossacks, 4
Council of Chalcedon, 92
Council of Nicaea, 92
Crucifixion, 93–94
Cultural Revolution, 5, 16, 48
Czechoslovakia, 6

Dachau, 5
Darwin, Charles, 14
Darwinism, 16, 24
da Vinci, Leonardo, 24
"A Dearth of Feeling" (Applebaum),
    79
death camps, xvi, 5, 22
de Gaulle, Charles, 83
democracy, Nazism and, 76
Democracy and Totalitarianism
    (Aron), 27
Democritus, 14
deportation, 5–7
Destruction of the European Jews, The
    (Hilberg), 2
dokhodiaga, 6
Dora, 5
Dostoyevsky, Fyodor, 25, 58, 65
Drang nach Osten, 77

Egypt, 62
Eichmann, Adolf, xix, 23–24
Einaudi, xvi
Einsatzgruppen, 4, 22
English Revolution, 69
Enlightenment, 14, 24, 42, 65
Erofeev, Venedikt, 34
Essence of Christianity, The
    (Harnack), 62
Ethiopia, 5, 9
eugenics, 16
Euripides, 77
evil
    Christianity and, 73, 85
    communism and, 54, 76
    definition of, 53–54
    incomprehensibility and,
        54–55
    insanity and, 55–56
    Judaism and, 85
    Nazism and, 54
    private property as, 2–3, 95
    will to, 54, 57
Exodus, 65
expropriation, 2–3
extermination of Jews
    concentration and, 3–4
    deportation and, 5–7
    expropriation and, 2–3
    Hitler, Adolf and, 22
    mobile slaughter operations
        and, 4–5
    sequence of events in, 1–11
    torture and, 11

Fackenheim, Emil, 86
famine, 9, 97–98
fascism, 34, 76, 86, 89, 98
Faulhaber, Cardinal, 86

Federov, 59
Fénelon, 64
Fessar, Gaston, 91
Final Solution, 4, 18–20, 87, 90
Finkielkraut, Alain, 84
forced-labor camps, xvi, 5, 6, 7
France
    anti-Semitism in, 83
    God and, 63
    Nazism in, 76
    Shoah, uniqueness of and, xv,
        80, 82
    Vichy, 82, 102
Franco, Francisco, 100
Führer Principle, 41
Furet, François, 82

genocide, 77–78
German Democratic Republic, 4
Germany, Nazification of, 16
Gestapo, 4, 22
gnosticism, 25, 41, 66–68
Gobineau, 61
God
    France and, 63
    relationship of Jews to, 61–63,
        84–85
Great Leap Forward, 5, 48
Great Purge, 5, 34, 50
The Great Terror, 8–9
Grenada, 51
Grosser, Alfred, 97
gulag, 6, 7, 98
Gulag Archipelago, The
    (Solzhenitsyn), xxi

Hadrian, xviii, 93
Haffner, Sebastien, 44

Halévy, Elie, 98–99
Harnack, Adolph von, 62–63
Hegel, Georg Wilhelm Frederick,
    14, 21, 24, 25, 61–62, 65
Heidegger, Martin, 15
Heraclitus, 13
Herder, Johann Gottfried, 14
heresies
    gnosticism, 66–68
    Marcionism, 66
    millenarianism, 66, 68–69
Herod the Great, xviii
heroism, 18
High Middle Ages, German, 77
Hilberg, Raul, 2, 4, 22
Himmler, Heinrich, 17–20, 22
History of European Socialism
    (Halévy), 98
Hitler, Adolf, xx, 14, 21, 43
    anti-Semitism of, 63
    atheism of, 63
    Catholic Church and, 89
    extermination camps and, 22
    genocide and, 78
    The Great Terror and, 9
    Nazism and, xiii, 21
    race, spirit of and, 48
    Stalin, Joseph alliance with,
        43–46, 99
    Versailles, Treaty of and, 90
Hitler-Stalin Pact, 99
Hobbes, Thomas, 34
Ho Chi Minh, 14
Holocaust denial, 76
    See also Shoah
Homer, 68
honor, 11
Hugo, Victor, 96
humanitarianism, 65, 86
L'Humanité, 37

Hungary, 88
Hutus, 79

Iagoda, Guenrikh, 75
ideology
    of communism, xv, 25, 28
    extermination and, 19
    genocide and, 77
    insanity and, 56
    language of, 14, 32
    of Lenin, Vladimir, 21
    of Nazism, xv, 22
    of Stalin, Joseph, 21
If This Is a Man (Levi), xvi
India, 26
insanity, evil and, 55–56
Institut de France, 95, 105n1
international law, 23
Iranaeus, Saint, 66
irrationalism, 21
Isaac, Jules, 92
Isaiah, 64, 93
Islam, 64–65, 66
Israel, xviii–xix, 62–64, 82–84
Italian fascism, 89, 98

Jacob, 85
Jacobins, 97
Jews
    Christianity and, 69, 83, 84,
        87–92
    communism and, 75
    emancipation of, xvii
    French, 82
    identity of, xvii–xix, 80
    Israel, founding of and, xviii
    Jewishness and, xvii–xviii
    Nazism and, 3–4

Nuremberg trials and, xvii
patriotism of, xviii–xix
race, concept of and, xvii
relationship to God of, 61–63,
    84–85
sequence of events in
    extermination of, 1–11
Shoah, memory of and, xiv–xv,
    98
See also Judaism; Shoah
Job, 86, 98
John, Saint, 66
John Paul II, Pope, 88
Jonas, Hans, 86
Josephus, 93
Journet, 91
Judaism
    Bolshevism and, 44
    evil and, 85
    gnosticism and, 66
    as people, xvii
    as religion, xvii
    See also Jews; Shoah
judicial execution, 8–9
Junger, Ernst, 58
justice
    killing, mode of and, 10–11
    morality and, 26

Kaganovitch, Lazar, 75
Kant, Immanuel, 16, 21, 45, 64
Kaplan, Jacob, 92
Kapo, xvii
Kautsky, Karl, 102
Kazakhstan, 9
Kazaks, 101
KGB, 4
Khazars, 77
Khrushchev report, xix, xx

Kierkegaard, Soren, 65
Koestler, Arthur, 91
Kolakowski, Leszek, 51
kolkhoz, 9, 35
Kolyma, 6
Kommandos, 4
Korea, 5, 9, 31, 33
Kravchenko trial of 1948, xx
Kriegel, Annie, 79
Kristallnacht, 22
Kulaks, 5

Lager, 5
Lamennais, 65
Langevin, Paul, 15
Laogai, 7, 98
Law of Return, xviii
Leibniz, Gottfried Wilhelm, 65
Lenin, Vladimir, 5, 14
    capitalism, overthrow of and,
        30–31, 99
    communism and, xiii, 25, 96
    gnosticism and, 66–67
    historical inevitability and, 42
    ideology of, 19, 21
    leader cult and, 41
    political life, destruction of
        and, 46–47
Levi, Primo, xvi–xvii, 2, 6, 53
liberty, communism and, 26, 27
Louis, Saint, 83
Lucretius, 14
Lukács, Georg, 15
Luther, Martin, 63
Luxemburg, Rosa, 102

Machiavelli, Niccolò, 46
Majdanek, 1

Mandelstam, Osip, 53, 58
Mao Tse-tung, 14, 15, 48, 49, 50
Marcionism, 62, 63, 66, 67–68, 88
Maritain, Jacques, 91
Marx, Karl, 66
Marxism, 42
Marxism-Leninism, 15
    gnosticism and, 66
    intellectual geneology of,
        13–14
    salvation and, 58, 58–59
    as scientific, 31
Massacres of Korea, The (Picasso), 15
Mathiez, Albert, 98
Maurras, Charles, 83
Meleans, 77
Mémoire et L'Oubli, La (Memory
    and Oblivion; Grosser), 97
memory
    of Bolshevism, 95–103
    of communism, xiii–xiv, 71–
        75, 86, 100–101, 102
    of Nazism, xiii–xiv, xv, 75–86,
        86–92, 100–101, 102
    religion and, 71
    of Shoah, xiv–xv
messianism, 69
metaphysics, 15
Michelangelo, 24
millenarianism, 68–69
Milosz, Czeslaw, 58
Mit Brennender Sorge (Pius XI), 87
mobile slaughter operations, 4–5
Montesquieu, 42
moral destruction
    communism and, 24–26, 31,
        32–36
    good, falsification of and,
        17–24
    ineptitude and, 13–17

Nazism and, 17–24, 31
morality
    Bible and, 26
    of communism, 21, 24–26,
        26–30
    justice and, 26
    of Nazism, 19, 20–24, 30
Moses, 26, 81
Mussolini, Benito, 100

Napoleon, 82
Narodnik heroes, 25
nationalism, 15, 21, 23, 50
National Socialism
    communism, Bolshevik and,
        95–96
    goal of, 95
    as philanthropic, 96
naturalism, 21
Nazism
    anti-Semitism and, 61–63
    "biblicism" of, 61–64
    Catholic Church and, 87–92
    Christianity and, 17–18,
        86–92, 93
    decadence and, 24
    democracy and, 76
    evil and, 54
    in France, 76
    German society and, 23
    goal of, xiii, 43–46
    good, falsification of and,
        17–24, 29
    Hitler, Adolf and, xiii, 21
    ideology of, xv, 22
    intellectual geneology of,
        13–17
    Jews and, 3–4, 75–86
    Marcionism and, 68

memory of, xiii–xiv, xv, 71,
75–86, 86–92, 100–101,
102
moral destruction and, 17–24,
31
morality of, 19, 20–24, 30
as philanthropic, xiii, 96
physical destruction and, 22
political life, destruction of
and, 39–46, 48
power and, xv, 31–32, 57–58
progress and, 24–25
race, concept of and, 18, 20
religion, hatred of and, 56
right and left, struggle
between and, 98–99
salvation and, 59–60, 69
science and, 95–96
Nechaiev, Sergei, 25
NEP. *See* New Economic Policy
Neruda, Pablo, 15
Netherlands, 88
New Economic Policy (NEP), 4, 49
New Testament, 64, 67
New York Times, 51
Nicaea, Council of, 92
Nietzsche, Friedrich, 14, 16, 21,
61, 64
Night of the Long Knives (1934),
9, 48
nihilism, 21
Nolte, Ernst, 82
North Korea, 7, 50
Novalis, 14
Nuremberg trials, xvi–xvii, 21, 99

Old Testament, 64, 67, 81
original sin, 85
Orwell, George, 53, 58, 91, 102

paganism, 58, 71–72
pantragism, 24
Panza, Sancho, 83
Papon, Maurice, 83–86
patriotism, xviii–xix
Paul, Saint, 64
Peasant War (1919), 4
Pechenegs, 77
Péguy, Charles, 63
Pelagianism, 59, 69
Pelagius, 59
Petain, Philipe, 83
physical destruction
concentration and, 3–4
deportation and, 5–7
expropriation and, 2–3
famine and, 9, 97–98
judicial execution and, 8–9
killing, mode of and, 10–11
mobile slaughter operations
and, 4–5
name and anonymity and, 10
Nazism and, 22
Picasso, Pablo, 15
Pied Piper of Hamelin, 60
Pius XI, Pope, 87, 88–89
Pius XII, Pope, 87–89, 106–7n7
Platonov, Andrei, 53, 58
Plotinus, 53
Poland, 6, 31, 43, 87
populism, Russian, 24
power
communism and, xv, 31–32,
57–58
Nazism and, xv, 31–32, 57–58
preservation of, 31–32, 49
private property
communism and, 2
evil and, 95
Nazism and, 23

progress
    communism and, 24–25, 42
    Enlightenment and, 24, 42
    Nazism and, 24–25
    salvation and, 59
progressivism, 24
prokuratura, 8
Protestantism, 62–63
Punic Wars, 77

Rakosi, Matyas, 45
Ratzinger, Cardinal. *See* Benedict
    XVI, Pope
Rauschning, Hermann, 58, 63
Red Army, 4
Reich, 22, 41
religion
    hatred of, 56
    memory and, 71
    Shoah, uniqueness of and,
        81, 84
Renan, Ernest, 83
Romania, 7, 31
Romanticism, 42
Rousseau, Jean-Jacques, 24, 42, 65
Rousset, David, xx
Russell, Bertrand, 102
Rwanda, 79

Sabbatai Zevi, 69
Sainte-Beuve, Charles-Augustin, 83
Saint-Simon, Henri de, 42
Sakharov, Andrei, 35
salami tactics, 45
salvation, 58–60, 63, 69, 72
Sarmatians, 77
Sartre, Jean-Paul, xx
Schlinder's List, 23

Schmitt, Carl, 15
Scholastics, 53
Scholem, Gershom, xix
science, 95–96
scientific movement, 14
Scriptures. *See* Bible
Scythians, 77
Seelisberg Conference of 1947, 92
Se questo è un uomo (If This Is a
    Man; Levi), xvi
Shalamov, Varlam, 6
Shoah
    banalization of, 77
    as foundational event, xix
    France and, xv
    as genocide, 77
    historical consciousness and, xiv
    Jews and God and, 84–85
    memory of, xiv–xv, 98
    politics and, xv
    religion of, 84
    right and left, struggle
        between and, xv
    scientific study and, xv
    theological reflection on,
        85–86
    uniqueness of, xiv, xv, xvi,
        80–83, 93–94
Shylock, 81
Siberia, 4, 6, 7
sin, 73, 85
Slovakia, 88
Sobibor, 1
social Darwinism, 16
socialism
    capitalism and, 28, 90
    communism and, 3–4
    French, 24
    German, 24
    Soviet camps and, xx

Soloviev, Vladimir, 58
Solzhenitsyn, Aleksandr, xxi, 35, 58
Souvarine, Boris, 79, 91
Spartacus, 93
Speer, Albert, 21
Spinoza, Baruch, 43
SS, 17, 60, 91
Stalin, Joseph, xx, 14, 15, 25, 43
    evil and, 55
    genocide and, 79
    Great Purge of, 8–9, 34, 50
    The Great Terror and, 8–9
    history, spirit of and, 48
    Hitler, Adolf alliance with,
        43–46, 99
    ideology of, 21
    leader cult and, 41, 42
    as tyrant, 55–56
Stasi (Ministry for State Security), 4
Switzerland, 46
Syriac Apocalypse, 85

Taborites, 69
Taiping Rebellion, 72
Talmud, 80
Tartars, 5
Tchernychevsky, Nikolaï, 25
ten commandments, 26–27, 59
Their Morality and Ours (Trotsky),
    26
theology
    communist "biblicism" and,
        64–66
    demon and the person and,
        56–58
    of evil, 53–56
    heresies and, 66–69
    Nazi "biblicism" and, 61–64
    salvation and, 58–60

Shoah, uniqueness of and,
    xvi–xvii
Thucydides, 77
Tibetans, 101
Titus, xviii, 93
Tkatchev, 25
Tolstoy, Leo, 65
Torah, 64, 65, 80, 84
torture, 8, 11
Treaty of Versailles, 43, 90
Treblinka, xvi, 1, 7
Trojan War, 77
Trojan Women, The (Euripides), 77
Trotsky, Leon, 24, 26, 41, 42
Tutsis, 79

Ukraine, 4, 9, 97, 101
Ukrainian genocide of 1932-33,
    78–79
universalism, communism and, 21,
    30
utopia, 42–43, 85

Valentinus, 66
Vatican II, xviii, 92
Vendeans, 78
Versailles, Treaty of, 43, 90
Vichy France, 82, 102
Vietnam, 5, 7
Volksgeist (the spirit of the people),
    46
voluntarism, 43

Waffen-SS, 18, 22
Wagnerism, 46, 64
Warsaw ghetto, xix
Wehrmacht, 4, 22

Zazoubrine, Vladimir, 4
zek, 7
Zinoviev, Gregory, 34–35, 42, 58
Zionism, 80, 85

ABOUT THE AUTHOR AND TRANSLATORS

ALAIN BESANÇON has taught at the École des hautes études en sciences sociales and is currently a member of the Academy of Moral and Political Sciences of the Institut de France. A specialist in Russian politics and intellectual history, he is the author of *The Forbidden Image: An Intellectual History of Iconoclasm* and *The Falsification of the Good: Soloviev and Orwell*. This is his fourth book to appear in English.

RALPH C. HANCOCK is Professor of Political Science at Brigham Young University. He also translated Philippe Bénéton's *Equality by Default* for ISI Books' Crosscurrents series.

NATHANIEL H. HANCOCK holds degrees in French translation and French literature from the Monterey Institute of International Studies and Brigham Young University.